Southern Living.

The
SOUTHERN
HERITAGE
COOKBOOK
LIBRARY

MOLASSES

CONTAINS
SULPHUR
DIOXIDE.

The SOUTHERN HERITAGE
Cookie Jar
COOKBOOK

OXMOOR HOUSE
Birmingham, Alabama

Southern Living

The Southern Heritage Cookbook Library

Copyright 1985 by Oxmoor House, Inc.
Book Division of Southern Progress Corporation
P.O. Box 2463, Birmingham, Alabama 35201

Southern Living® is a federally registered trademark belonging to
Southern Living, Inc.

Library of Congress Catalog Number: 85-060120
ISBN: 0-8487-0616-1

Manufactured in the United States of America

The Southern Heritage COOKIE JAR Cookbook

Executive Editor: Ann H. Harvey
Southern Living® Foods Editor: Jean W. Liles
Senior Editor: Joan E. Denman
Senior Foods Editor: Katherine M. Eakin
Assistant Editor: Ellen de Lathouder
Assistant Foods Editor: Helen R. Turk
Director, Test Kitchen: Laura N. Massey
Test Kitchen Home Economists: Kay E. Clarke, Rebecca J. Riddle,
   Elizabeth J. Taliaferro, Dee Waller, Elise Wright Walker
Production Manager: Jerry R. Higdon
Copy Editor: Melinda E. West
Editorial Assistants: Mary Ann Laurens, Karen P. Traccarella
Food Photographer: Jim Bathie
Food Stylist: Sara Jane Ball
Layout Designer: Christian von Rosenvinge
Mechanical Artist: Faith Nance
Research Editors: Alicia Hathaway, Philip Napoli

Special Consultants

Art Director: Irwin Glusker
Heritage Consultant: Meryle Evans
Foods Writer: Lillian B. Marshall
Food and Recipe Consultants: Marilyn Wyrick Ingram,
   Audrey P. Stehle

Cover (clockwise from front): Decorator Sugar Cookies (page 58),
Butterscotch-Fruit Squares (page 91) and Hello Dolly Bars (page 92),
Holiday Gingerbread Bears (page 136), Pecan Sandies (page 77),
Fruitcake Cookies (page 117), Spritz Cookies (page 86), Madeleines
(page 29), Chocolate Sandwich Cookies (page 62), and Citrus
Wafers (page 69).

Collection of Bonnie Slotnick

CONTENTS

INTRODUCTION

From childhood into old age, from Macaroons to Hello Dollies, Southerners have a special affinity for the well-filled cookie jar. Cookies have many prefixes, such as *milk and-*, *tea and-*, even *champagne and-*. We embrace them all. Were there tea cakes in Richard Pynson's first cookbook to be printed in English in the 1500s? The sole surviving copy is owned by the Marquise of Bath, so we cannot be certain. But we may infer that there were; the Greeks and Romans had mixed seeds with honey to make cakes.

Samuel Pepys made careful note of his first taste of "tee, a China drink" in 1660, arguably accompanied by cakes. For, much as we quote Hannah Glasse, the fact is that, from the publication of Sir Hugh Plat's *Delightes for Ladies* in 1600, there had been a steady flow of cookbooks in England. Most of them were by professionals for professionals; cakes were part of their stock in trade. Glasse's great contribution, nearly 150 years later, was to write for the amateur cook.

The English settlers left home with a repertoire of cakes in their minds and hearts, but they had no chance to practice what they knew until danger subsided and ingredients became available. Their penchant for heavy spicing was tempered over time, and tastes were broadened by contact with other European cultures. From early on, the South enjoyed ocean commerce with the Dutch of New Amsterdam, now Manhattan, and with Pennsylvanians, many of whom were German — *Deutsch*, which sounded like Dutch to the English. By 1683, there were Swedes, Irish, Scots, and Welsh in Pennsylvania. There was some resettling southward from the upper and middle colonies.

The Dutch, the South soon learned, had a long-handled iron to make wafers; they formed ginger cakes in moulds, and fried a sweet cake that Mary Randolph was to call "Dough-Nut, a Yankee Cake" in *The Virginia Housewife*, 1824. Huguenots and Moravians came into the Carolinas; Germans and Scandinavians coexisted with Mexicans in Texas, all finding common ground in their love for sweet cakes. The Greeks found the Spanish in Florida; they exchanged recipes, as did the French with the Spanish in Louisiana. Sharing serves to reinforce traditions; the rich variety of Southern cookies is ample proof.

COLONIAL 'CAKES'

C olonial cooks had never known a time when they didn't have almonds and ginger. Almonds were mentioned in print in fourteenth-century England, centuries before Hannah Glasse's "mackeroon" recipe appeared in 1796. When we buy blanched almonds and toss them into a food processor or, even more decadently, open a can of almond paste, we may hear echoes of earlier instructions to blanch the almonds, rub the skins off with a rough towel, and pound heavily with mortar and pestle to reduce the nuts to paste. Eliza Leslie's *New Cookery Book*, 1857, states that macaroons can also be made with "ground-nuts" (peanuts); Americanization had set in.

The Romans knew ginger, and it was used in Europe during the days of the Empire. But when Marco Polo reintroduced it from Asia, interest in ginger reached a fever pitch; early recipes for ginger cakes call for large amounts of it. In England, ginger cakes were sweetened with treacle, sugar, or honey. In the New World, sugar was dear and honey scarce. Then, early in the 1700s, molasses arrived, made a hasty marriage with ginger, and the American ginger cake was born. William Byrd, the eminent food faddist of Westover, craved it daily, and it was whispered that Virginia politicians used ginger cakes to buy votes.

"Kisses for a Slack Oven"—people had a knack for naming recipes in the eighteenth century—were crisp little meringue "cakes." We don't call them cakes now, but meringues are still baked in a slack, or barely warm, oven. One of Eliza Leslie's most imaginative flights was to form kisses like half-eggs and then bake them only until done on the outside. After the soft "innards" were hollowed out, she instructed her readers to " . . . fill the vacancy with any sort of stiff jelly. . . . Clap two halves together and unite them at the edges with a little of the leftover meringue."

Jumbles, spelled *jumbals* by the English (from the Old English *gimbal*, meaning ring), were originally shaped into strips and joined at the ends to form rings or knots. They later became drop or rolled cookies. These, along with tea cakes such as Naples biscuits (ladyfingers) and shortbread from Scotland and northern England, comprised the main body of sweet cakes that the settlers knew well.

Currants dot Mary Telfair's Derby Cakes (front) which, along with Ladyfingers (rear), Gingersnaps, and Coconut Macaroons (center), were colonial favorites.

KISSES AND MACAROONS

KISS CAKES

3 egg whites
½ cup sugar
⅛ teaspoon lemon extract

Beat egg whites (at room temperature) in a medium mixing bowl until foamy. Gradually add sugar, 1 tablespoon at a time, beating until stiff peaks form. Fold in lemon extract.

Drop by heaping teaspoonfuls 2 inches apart onto waxed paper-lined cookie sheets. Bake at 300° for 45 minutes. Cool slightly on cookie sheets; gently remove from waxed paper. Yield: 4 dozen.

PECAN KISS CAKES

4 egg whites
1½ cups sugar
1 teaspoon vanilla extract
1 cup chopped pecans

Beat egg whites (at room temperature) in a medium mixing bowl until foamy; add sugar, 2 tablespoons at a time, beating until stiff peaks form. Fold in vanilla and pecans.

Drop by heaping teaspoonfuls 2 inches apart onto waxed paper-lined cookie sheets. Bake at 250° for 55 minutes. Remove from waxed paper, and cool on wire racks. Yield: about 8 dozen.

PRALINE KISSES

1 egg white
1 cup firmly packed brown sugar
1 teaspoon vanilla extract
1½ cups finely chopped pecans

Beat egg white (at room temperature) in a medium mixing bowl until foamy. Gradually add sugar, 1 tablespoon at a time, beating until stiff peaks form and sugar dissolves. Fold in vanilla and pecans.

Drop by heaping teaspoonfuls 3 inches apart onto ungreased cookie sheets. Bake at 225° for 1½ hours. Turn oven off; cool cookies in oven at least 1 hour. (Do not open oven door.) Remove from cookie sheets, and serve immediately, or store in airtight containers. Yield: about 3½ dozen.

CHOCOLATE-NUT KISSES

2 egg whites
½ cup powdered sugar
1 tablespoon cocoa
Dash of salt
½ cup chopped pecans

Beat egg whites (at room temperature) in a medium mixing bowl until stiff peaks form. Gradually sift sugar, cocoa, and salt over surface of egg whites; gently fold into egg whites. Fold in pecans.

Drop by heaping teaspoonfuls 1 inch apart onto well-greased cookie sheets. Bake at 300° for 35 minutes. Cool slightly on cookie sheets. Gently remove from cookie sheets, and cool completely on wire racks. Store in an airtight container. Yield: 2½ dozen.

In this lithograph, Kiss Me Quick, *Currier and Ives displayed more than their usual sense of humor, c.1860.*

Chocolate Chip Forgotten Cookies are baked in the old "baking-day" way, when kisses were baked last as the oven cooled.

CHOCOLATE CHIP FORGOTTEN COOKIES

2 egg whites
Dash of salt
⅔ cup sugar
½ teaspoon vanilla extract
1 (6-ounce) package
  semisweet chocolate
  morsels
1 cup chopped pecans

Preheat oven to 350°. Beat egg whites (at room temperature) in a large mixing bowl until foamy; add salt. Gradually add sugar, 1 tablespoon at a time, beating until stiff peaks form. Fold in vanilla, chocolate morsels, and pecans.

Drop by heaping teaspoonfuls 2 inches apart onto aluminum foil-lined cookie sheets. Place in oven, and immediately turn off heat. Do not open oven door for at least 12 hours. Gently remove cookies from aluminum foil, and store in an airtight container. Yield: about 3 dozen.

BREADCRUMB MERINGUE COOKIES

4 egg whites
Dash of salt
2 cups sugar
1 cup fine dry breadcrumbs
1 cup finely chopped pecans
1 teaspoon vanilla extract

Beat egg whites (at room temperature) in a medium mixing bowl until foamy; add salt. Gradually add sugar, 1 tablespoon at a time, beating until stiff peaks form. Fold in breadcrumbs, pecans, and vanilla.

Drop by heaping teaspoonfuls 2 inches apart onto waxed paper-lined cookie sheets. Bake at 350° for 15 minutes. Remove from waxed paper, and cool on wire racks. Yield: 7 dozen.

Thomas Jefferson

Mary Randolph

MONTICELLO MACAROONS

1 pound blanched almonds, finely ground
2¾ cups sifted powdered sugar
3 egg whites

Combine almonds and sugar in a large mixing bowl; mix well. Gradually add egg whites (at room temperature), stirring until well blended.

Drop by teaspoonfuls 2 inches apart onto parchment-lined cookie sheets. Bake at 300° for 20 minutes or until lightly browned. Remove from parchment, and cool on wire racks. Yield: 5 dozen.

S ir Hugh Plat's 1600 recipe "To make a Marchpane" (marzipan, the foundation of macaroons) was already old when written, and predates Mrs. Glasse's version by a century and a half. Plat used it to fill fancy cakes: "When your [almond] paste is beaten fine, drive it thin with a rowling pin, and so lay it on a bottome of wafers," he wrote. When grinding almonds, he added rose water to keep the nuts from oiling, a technique no doubt used by Mary Randolph and by Jefferson's cooks at Monticello in the 1800s.

MARY RANDOLPH'S MACAROONS

1 (8-ounce) can almond paste
¾ cup sifted powdered sugar
¼ teaspoon almond extract
2 egg whites
¼ cup all-purpose flour
¼ teaspoon baking powder
⅛ teaspoon salt
2 tablespoons sugar

Combine paste, ¾ cup sugar, and almond extract in a large mixing bowl; beat well. Add egg whites (at room temperature), mixing well. Combine flour, baking powder, and salt in a small mixing bowl. Add to almond mixture, blending well.

Drop by heaping teaspoonfuls 2 inches apart onto parchment-lined cookie sheets. Flatten center of each cookie with the back of a wet teaspoon; sprinkle lightly with 2 tablespoons sugar. Let cookies stand 2 hours at room temperature.

Bake at 300° for 25 to 30 minutes. Cool slightly on cookie sheets. Remove from parchment, and cool completely on wire racks. Yield: about 2 dozen.

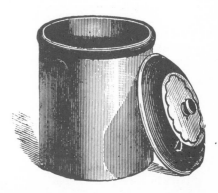

New Bern Almond Macaroons, named for the city settled by the Swiss in 1710.

CAKE-CRUMB MACAROONS

1 egg white
½ cup sifted powdered sugar, divided
½ teaspoon almond extract
2 cups fine cake crumbs (pound, yellow, or white)

Beat egg white (at room temperature) in a medium mixing bowl until soft peaks form; gradually add 2 tablespoons powdered sugar, beating until stiff peaks form. Add almond extract, beating until well blended. Fold in remaining powdered sugar and cake crumbs.

Drop by heaping teaspoonfuls 2 inches apart onto greased cookie sheets. Bake at 300° for 20 minutes or until lightly browned. Remove from cookie sheets, and cool on wire racks. Store cookies in airtight containers. Yield: 2½ dozen.

PASSOVER MACAROONS

Vegetable oil
2 teaspoons matzo meal, divided
2 egg whites
½ cup sugar
1 cup blanched almonds, finely ground

Grease cookie sheet with oil; sprinkle with 1 teaspoon matzo meal. Set aside.

Beat egg whites (at room temperature) in a medium mixing bowl until foamy. Gradually add sugar, beating until stiff peaks form. Fold in almonds and remaining matzo meal.

Drop mixture by teaspoonfuls 1 inch apart onto prepared cookie sheet. Bake at 300° for 20 minutes or until lightly browned. Remove from cookie sheet, and cool on a wire rack. Yield: 2 dozen.

NEW BERN ALMOND MACAROONS

1 (8-ounce) can almond paste
½ cup sugar
1 teaspoon vanilla extract
2 egg whites
18 maraschino cherries, drained and halved

Combine almond paste, sugar, and vanilla in a large mixing bowl. Add egg whites (at room temperature), and beat until smooth. Chill dough at least 2 hours.

Place chilled dough in container of a cookie press fitted with a star tip. Press rosettes 2 inches apart onto lightly greased cookie sheets. Bake at 325° for 25 minutes. Remove from oven; top each cookie with a cherry half. Remove from cookie sheets, and cool on wire racks. Store in airtight containers. Yield: about 3 dozen.

COCONUT MACAROONS

2 egg whites
1 cup sifted powdered sugar
1 (3½-ounce) can flaked
coconut
1 teaspoon vanilla extract
Dash of salt

Beat egg whites (at room temperature) in a medium mixing bowl until stiff but not dry; fold in sugar, 2 tablespoons at a time. Fold in coconut, vanilla, and salt.

Drop by teaspoonfuls onto parchment-lined cookie sheets. Bake at 300° for 30 minutes. Gently remove from parchment, and cool on wire racks. Yield: 3 dozen.

OATMEAL-COCONUT MACAROONS

1 cup shortening
1 cup sugar
1 cup firmly packed brown
sugar
2 eggs, well beaten
1 teaspoon vanilla extract
1 cup all-purpose flour
1 teaspoon baking soda
½ teaspoon salt
4 cups regular oats, uncooked
1 cup flaked coconut

Cream shortening in a large mixing bowl; gradually add sugar, beating well. Stir in eggs and vanilla.

Combine flour, soda, and salt in a small mixing bowl; add flour mixture to creamed mixture, stirring well. Stir in oats and coconut.

Shape dough into 1-inch balls; place 2 inches apart on greased cookie sheets. Bake at 375° for 10 to 12 minutes. Remove from cookie sheets, and cool on wire racks. Yield: 5½ dozen.

The young ladies in this 1890s trade card are enjoying teatime, complete with cookies and an airy setting.

BRAZIL NUT MACAROONS

2 cups Brazil nuts, coarsely
chopped
1 cup firmly packed light
brown sugar
1 cup firmly packed dark
brown sugar
2 egg whites
⅛ teaspoon salt
1 teaspoon vanilla extract

Combine nuts and sugar in container of an electric blender; process until mixture resembles coarse meal. Set aside.

Combine egg whites (at room temperature) and salt in a large mixing bowl; beat until stiff but not dry. Fold in nut-sugar mixture and vanilla.

Drop by teaspoonfuls onto aluminum foil-lined cookie sheets. Bake at 325° for 10 minutes. Cool completely on cookie sheets. Remove from aluminum foil to serve. Yield: 6½ dozen.

DATE-NUT MACAROONS

1 (8-ounce) package chopped
dates
1 cup chopped pecans
1 cup sifted powdered sugar,
divided
2 egg whites
½ teaspoon vanilla extract

Combine dates, pecans, and ½ cup sugar in a small mixing bowl. Set aside.

Beat egg whites (at room temperature) in a medium mixing bowl until soft peaks form. Add remaining sugar, 2 tablespoons at a time, beating until stiff peaks form. Fold in reserved date mixture.

Drop date mixture by heaping teaspoonfuls onto greased cookie sheets. Bake at 200° for 1 hour. Cool slightly on cookie sheets. Remove to wire racks to cool completely. Yield: about 5 dozen.

SHORTBREAD AND GINGER COOKIES

SHORTBREAD

1 cup unsalted butter,
   softened
¾ cup firmly packed dark
   brown sugar
2 cups all-purpose flour
¾ teaspoon salt

Cream butter in a medium mixing bowl; gradually add sugar, beating until light and fluffy. Add flour and salt; stir until well blended. Divide dough into three equal portions; chill at least 1 hour.

Press one portion of dough into a 7- x 5-inch rectangle on a lightly greased cookie sheet; press with tines of a fork around outer edge of rectangle. Divide rectangle into 2½- x 1-inch bars by making deep indentions with a wooden pick. Repeat procedure with remaining portions of dough.

Bake at 300° for 30 minutes; cool slightly. Break warm shortbread into bars. Remove from cookie sheets, and cool completely on wire racks. Yield: 3½ dozen.

Note: Chilled dough may be pressed into a floured shortbread mold and turned out onto a lightly greased cookie sheet. Bake as directed.

Shortbread formed in wooden mold, ready to trim and bake.

How can a few simple ingredients come together to make a treat as good as shortbread? As generations of Scots can attest, that magic triplicity of butter, sugar, and flour can even make a nation proud. There is no magic without butter. We dare not tamper with tradition there, but we may choose the shape of the cakes. For a party tray, fans may be choicest for looks, but any shape will do if it is shortbread.

SHORTBREAD FANS

1 cup butter, softened
½ cup sugar
2½ cups all-purpose flour

Cream butter in a small mixing bowl; gradually add sugar, beating until light and fluffy. Gradually add flour, stirring until thoroughly blended. Divide dough into 4 equal portions; pat each portion into a 5-inch circle on lightly greased cookie sheets.

Score the surface of each circle into 8 wedges with a wooden pick. Press around the outer edge of each circle with tines of a fork.

Bake at 325° for 25 minutes or until lightly browned. Remove from oven; make deep indentions along the scored lines. Cool completely on cookie sheets. Break into wedges to serve. Yield: 32 wedges.

DUTCH BUTTER COOKIES

1 cup butter, softened
1 cup sugar
1 egg
2 cups all-purpose flour

Cream butter in a medium mixing bowl; gradually add sugar, beating until light and fluffy. Add egg, and beat well. Gradually stir in flour. (Dough will be sticky.)

Divide dough in half. Place each portion of dough in well-greased 8-inch square pans. With floured hands, press dough into pans.

Place pans in a cold oven. Bake at 350° for 20 minutes or until lightly browned.

Remove from oven, and cut into 2-inch squares while warm. Remove from pans, and cool on wire racks. Yield: about 3 dozen.

SHORTBREAD COOKIES

1 cup all-purpose flour
½ cup powdered sugar
½ cup cornstarch
1 cup butter, softened

Sift together flour, sugar, and cornstarch in a small mixing bowl; set aside.

Cream butter; gradually stir in reserved flour mixture. Shape dough into a ball, and chill 1 to 2 hours.

Shape dough into 1-inch balls, and place 2 inches apart on ungreased cookie sheets. Press a lightly floured fork in center of each ball to flatten to ½-inch thickness. Bake at 300° for 20 to 22 minutes. Cool slightly on cookie sheets; remove from cookie sheets, and cool completely on wire racks. Yield: 4 dozen.

ALMOND SHORTBREAD

1 cup butter, softened
1 cup sugar
1 egg yolk
1 teaspoon almond extract
2 cups all-purpose flour
1 cup blanched almonds, finely ground

Cream butter in a large mixing bowl; gradually add sugar, beating until light and fluffy. Add egg yolk; beat well. Stir in almond extract. Gradually add flour and ground almonds, stirring until well blended.

Press dough into a lightly greased 13- x 9- x 2-inch baking pan. Bake at 325° for 40 minutes or until lightly browned. Cut into 2-inch squares. Cool in pan 10 minutes; remove to wire racks to cool completely. Yield: 2 dozen.

Butter-making class at Hampton Institute, founded in Virginia, 1868. Photograph c.1900.

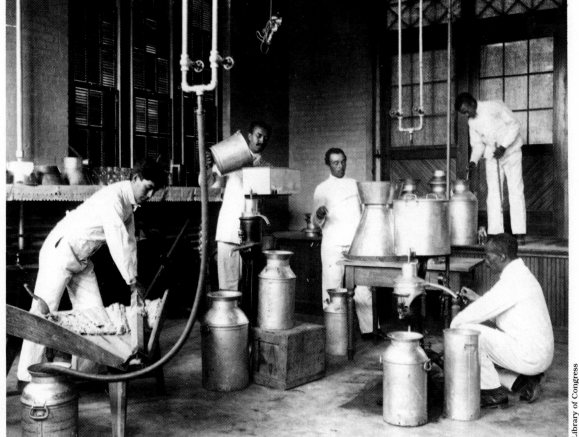

SHORTBREAD SURPRISE COOKIES

2 cups butter, softened
¾ cup firmly packed
 brown sugar
2 teaspoons vanilla extract
5 cups all-purpose flour
3½ cups pecan halves
Powdered sugar

Cream butter in a large mixing bowl; gradually add brown sugar, beating well. Add vanilla; mix well. Gradually add flour, 1 cup at a time, stirring until well blended.

Shape dough into 1-inch balls, inserting one pecan half into center of each ball. Place cookies 2 inches apart on greased cookie sheets. Bake at 375° for 12 minutes or until lightly browned. Remove from cookie sheets, and cool on wire racks. Roll in powdered sugar. Yield: about 16 dozen.

Note: Cookies may be frozen before rolling in powdered sugar.

SWEDISH RYE COOKIES

1 cup butter, softened
⅓ cup sugar
1¼ cups all-purpose flour
1¼ cups rye flour

Cream butter in a large mixing bowl; gradually add sugar, beating until light and fluffy. Add flour, stirring well. (It may be necessary to work flour into dough using hands.) Cover with plastic wrap, and chill slightly.

Turn dough out onto a lightly floured surface; roll to ⅛-inch thickness. Prick entire surface of dough with tines of a fork; cut with a 2½-inch cookie cutter. Make a hole just off center in each cookie using a ½-inch cookie cutter.

Place 2 inches apart on lightly greased cookie sheets. Bake at 350° for 10 minutes. Remove from cookie sheets, and cool on wire racks. Yield: about 4 dozen.

Note: Leftover cookies may be placed in an airtight container and frozen for later use.

TRYON PALACE GINGER COOKIES

⅔ cup vegetable oil
1¼ cups sugar, divided
1 egg
¼ cup molasses
2 cups all-purpose flour
2 teaspoons baking soda
½ teaspoon salt
1 teaspoon ground ginger
1 teaspoon ground cinnamon

Combine oil and 1 cup sugar in a large mixing bowl; beat at medium speed of an electric mixer until well blended. Add egg, and beat well. Gradually stir in molasses.

Sift together flour, soda, salt, ginger, and cinnamon in a medium mixing bowl; gradually add to creamed mixture, stirring well after each addition.

Place remaining sugar in a small mixing bowl; drop dough by teaspoonfuls into sugar, rolling to coat well.

Place balls 3 inches apart on lightly greased cookie sheets. Bake at 350° for 8 to 10 minutes. (Cookies will flatten and crinkle.) Cool slightly on cookie sheets. Remove from cookie sheets, and cool completely on wire racks. Store in airtight containers. Yield: about 5½ dozen.

Tryon Palace is the centerpiece of a thirteen-acre garden complex which includes the restored Stanley House and other historical landmarks.

Tryon Palace

OLD-FASHIONED GINGER SNAPS

¾ cup shortening
1½ cups sugar, divided
1 egg
¼ cup molasses
2½ cups all-purpose flour
2 teaspoons baking soda
2 teaspoons ground ginger
2 teaspoons ground cinnamon
2 teaspoon ground cloves

Cream shortening in a large mixing bowl; gradually add 1 cup sugar, beating well. Add egg; beat well. Stir in molasses.

Sift together flour, soda, ginger, cinnamon, and cloves in a medium mixing bowl. Gradually add to creamed mixture, stirring well. Chill 2 hours.

Shape dough into 1-inch balls. Dip half of each ball in remaining sugar. Place balls, sugar side up, 2 inches apart on lightly greased cookie sheets. Flatten balls with the bottom of a glass. Bake at 350° for 12 minutes or until browned. (Tops will crack.) Remove from cookie sheets, and cool on wire racks. Yield: about 4½ dozen.

William Tryon, 1729-1788, appointed Lieutenant Governor of North Carolina by the Crown, arrived in the colonial capital of New Bern in 1764. He succeeded Governor Dobbs in 1765. Working with English surveyor-architect John Hawks, he built the English-style Tryon Palace in 1770. Hawks' original plans were logged in the Public Records Office in London and were invaluable in the restoration of the building, which was destroyed by fire in 1798. In 1771, Tryon served as Governor of New York and then returned to England. When General Howe took New York, Tryon returned to command a corps of Loyalists in the New York district, returning to England in 1780. While Tryon remained a British Loyalist, his handsome palace became a treasured piece of Americana.

WINKLER'S GINGER CAKES

4 cups molasses
¾ cup shortening
1 teaspoon baking soda
1 cup buttermilk
10 cups all-purpose flour
¼ teaspoon ground ginger
¼ teaspoon ground cinnamon
¼ teaspoon ground cloves
Brown Sugar Water (optional)

Combine molasses and shortening in a large mixing bowl, beating well. Add soda to buttermilk, stirring until soda dissolves; add to molasses mixture, mixing well.

Sift together flour, ginger, cinnamon, and cloves in a large mixing bowl; gradually add to molasses mixture, stirring well after each addition. Cover and refrigerate overnight.

Roll a small portion of dough to ½-inch thickness on a lightly floured surface, keeping remaining dough chilled until ready to use. Cut into 5- x 2-inch strips. Place on lightly greased cookie sheets.

Bake cookies at 350° for 15 minutes. Remove from cookie sheets, and cool on wire racks; brush with Brown Sugar Water, if desired. Repeat procedure with remaining dough. Yield: about 3 dozen.

Brown Sugar Water:

½ cup firmly packed brown sugar
½ cup water

Combine sugar and water in a small mixing bowl; mix well. Brush over tops of cookies. Yield: about ½ cup.

MORAVIAN GINGER COOKIES

½ cup butter, softened
¼ cup shortening
¾ cup firmly packed brown sugar
2 cups dark molasses
1 tablespoon baking soda
¼ cup boiling water
7½ cups all-purpose flour, divided
1 teaspoon salt
2 tablespoons ground ginger
2 tablespoons ground cinnamon
2 tablespoons ground cloves

Cream butter and shortening in a large mixing bowl; beat until well blended. Add sugar and molasses, beating well.

Dissolve soda in water, stirring well. Sift together 2 cups flour, salt, ginger, cinnamon, and cloves in a medium mixing bowl; add to creamed mixture alternately with dissolved soda, beginning and ending with flour-spice mixture. Stir well after each addition. Gradually add enough remaining flour to make a moderately stiff dough; stir after each addition until well blended.

Divide dough in half; wrap each half in waxed paper, and chill overnight.

Remove waxed paper from one portion of dough; let stand at room temperature about 10 minutes. (Keep remaining dough chilled until ready to use.) Roll dough to ⅛-inch thickness on a well-floured surface; cut with a fluted 2½-inch cookie cutter. Place 2 inches apart on greased cookie sheets. Bake at 375° for 6 minutes. Remove from cookie sheets, and cool on wire racks. Repeat procedure with remaining dough. Yield: about 10 dozen.

Cutting cookies at Winkler Bakery.

Moravian Ginger Cookies (center) and Moravian Tea Cakes (page 27) displayed on the original table at Winkler Bakery, Old Salem, North Carolina.

JUMBLES AND TEA CAKES

CINNAMON JUMBLES

½ teaspoon baking soda
¾ cup buttermilk
½ cup shortening
1¼ cups sugar, divided
1 egg
1 teaspoon vanilla extract
2 cups all-purpose flour
¼ teaspoon salt
1 teaspoon ground cinnamon

Dissolve soda in buttermilk; stir well, and set aside.

Cream shortening in a large mixing bowl; gradually add 1 cup sugar, beating well. Add egg; beat well. Stir in reserved buttermilk mixture and vanilla.

Combine flour and salt in a medium mixing bowl; gradually stir into creamed mixture. Chill dough 2 hours.

Combine remaining ¼ cup sugar and cinnamon in a small mixing bowl. Set aside.

Drop by teaspoonfuls 2 inches apart onto lightly greased cookie sheets. Sprinkle with reserved sugar mixture. Bake at 375° for 8 to 10 minutes. Remove from cookie sheets, and cool on wire racks. Yield: about 4 dozen.

JUBILEE JUMBLES

½ cup shortening
½ cup sugar
1 cup firmly packed brown sugar
2 eggs
1 teaspoon vanilla extract
2¾ cups all-purpose flour
½ teaspoon baking soda
½ teaspoon salt
1 cup evaporated milk
1 cup chopped pecans
Burnt Butter Glaze

Cream shortening in a large mixing bowl; gradually add sugar, beating well. Add eggs, one at a time, beating well after each addition. Stir in vanilla.

Sift together flour, soda, and salt; add to creamed mixture alternately with milk, beginning and ending with flour mixture. Stir well after each addition. Stir in pecans. Cover and chill at least 1 hour.

Drop by teaspoonfuls 2 inches apart onto greased cookie sheets. Bake at 375° for 8 to 10 minutes. Remove from cookie sheets, and cool on wire racks. Spoon Burnt Butter Glaze over cookies. Cool completely. Yield: about 3 dozen.

Burnt Butter Glaze:

2 tablespoons butter
2 cups sifted powdered sugar
¼ cup evaporated milk

Place butter in a heavy saucepan. Cook over low heat until golden brown, stirring frequently. Remove from heat; gradually add sugar, beating well. Add milk; beat until mixture is slightly thickened. Use immediately. Yield: about 1 cup.

The manuscript recipe for "Jumbles," reproduced above, although dated 1846, still uses the original ring or "gimbal" shaping. No estimate is given for yield, but almost four pounds of dough yields a lot of cookies. With canisters of ingredients, a scale to weigh them with, and time to form the cakes, the result would have to be a delicious and rather sizeable batch of jumbles. A pound of butter is worked to a cream with a pound of sugar. A pound of flour is mixed with six beaten eggs; then a "large tablespoonful" of cinnamon is beaten into the combined mixtures — a Herculean task considering the time it was written. Then "flour your hands. Make the dough into large rolls . . . and form them into rings by joining the ends nicely. Lay them in an oven [;] bake from five to ten minutes." These jumbles clearly have the basics for a tasty, traditional cookie.

Dropped Coconut Jumbles and round-cut Mocha Jumbles.

COCONUT JUMBLES

1 egg
1½ cups sugar
½ cup butter or margarine, melted
½ teaspoon baking soda
½ cup buttermilk
2½ cups all-purpose flour
2 cups flaked coconut
Additional sugar

Beat egg in a large mixing bowl until foamy. Gradually add 1½ cups sugar and butter, beating constantly

Dissolve soda in buttermilk; add to creamed mixture, beating well. Stir in flour and coconut. Cover and chill dough at least 1 hour.

Shape dough into 1-inch balls; roll in additional sugar. Place 2 inches apart on greased cookie sheets. Bake at 350° for 10 to 12 minutes. Remove from cookie sheets, and cool on wire racks. Yield: about 7 dozen.

MOCHA JUMBLES

½ (4-ounce) bar sweet baking chocolate
¼ cup butter or margarine, softened and divided
1 cup sugar
1 egg
2 tablespoons cold coffee
2 cups all-purpose flour
1½ teaspoons baking powder
¼ teaspoon ground cinnamon
Additional sugar

Combine chocolate and 1 tablespoon butter in top of a double boiler; place over simmering water until melted. Remove from heat, and set aside.

Cream remaining butter in a large mixing bowl; gradually add 1 cup sugar, beating well. Add egg, coffee, and reserved chocolate mixture; beat well.

Combine flour, baking powder, and cinnamon in a medium mixing bowl; stir into creamed mixture, mixing well. Chill dough at least 2 hours.

Turn dough out onto a lightly floured surface; roll to ¼-inch thickness. Cut with a floured doughnut cutter. Place 2 inches apart on lightly greased cookie sheets; sprinkle lightly with additional sugar. Bake at 350° for 12 minutes. Cool slightly on cookie sheets. Remove to wire racks to cool completely. Yield: about 1 dozen.

SUGAR

Sotterly was built in 1730 by George Plater in St. Marys County, Maryland.

SOTTERLY JUMBLES

1 cup butter, softened
2 cups sugar
4 eggs
¼ cup brandy
4½ cups all-purpose flour
1 teaspoon baking soda
½ teaspoon nutmeg

Cream butter in a large mixing bowl; gradually add sugar, beating well. Add eggs, one at a time, beating well. Stir in brandy, mixing well.

Sift together flour, soda, and nutmeg; add to creamed mixture, mixing well to form a soft dough. Chill 2 hours.

Turn dough out onto a lightly floured surface; roll to ¼-inch thickness. Cut with a 2-inch round cutter. Place 2 inches apart on ungreased cookies sheets. Bake at 350° for 15 minutes or until lightly browned. Remove from cookie sheets, and cool on wire racks. Yield: about 6 dozen.

O ne of the pre-Revolutionary architectural treasures of St. Marys County, Maryland, is Sotterly, built in 1730. George Plater built the home, and upon his death it passed to his son, who later became governor of Maryland. The grandson of the Governor eventually lost the estate at the gaming table to a Colonel Somerville. Colonel Thomas Barber subsequently bought the property. It was the Barber womenfolk who handed down the recipe for Sotterly Jumbles for the delectation of us all. In this recipe, the cookie is rolled and cut, just one of the many shapings possible for this ancient form of "cake."

WAVERLY JUMBLES

1 cup butter, softened
1½ cups firmly packed
  brown sugar
2 eggs
2 tablespoons rose water
3½ cups all-purpose flour
½ teaspoon ground nutmeg

Cream butter in a medium mixing bowl; gradually add sugar, beating until light and fluffy. Add eggs and rose water, beating well.

Sift together flour and nutmeg; add to creamed mixture, stirring until well blended. Chill dough at least 1 hour.

Shape dough into 1½-inch balls; roll each ball into an 8-inch rope. Shape each rope into a coil, and place 2 inches apart on greased cookie sheets. Bake at 350° for 12 to 15 minutes. Cool slightly on cookie sheets. Remove from cookie sheets, and cool completely on wire racks. Yield: about 4 dozen.

BUTTER TEA CAKES

1 cup butter, softened
1½ cups sugar
3 eggs
3 tablespoons whipping
cream
1 teaspoon vanilla extract
4 cups all-purpose flour
1 tablespoon baking powder

Cream butter in a large mixing bowl. Gradually add sugar; beat until light and fluffy. Add eggs; beat well. Add whipping cream and vanilla; beat well.

Combine flour and baking powder in a medium mixing bowl; stir well. Add to creamed mixture. Shape into a ball, and chill thoroughly.

Roll dough to ¼-inch thickness on a lightly floured surface. Cut with a 3-inch round cookie cutter. Place on lightly greased cookie sheets 2 inches apart; bake at 325° for 12 minutes or until edges are lightly browned. Remove from cookie sheets and cool completely on wire racks. Yield: about 4 dozen.

DROP TEA CAKES

1 cup butter or margarine,
softened
1 cup vegetable oil
1 cup sugar
2 eggs
2 teaspoons vanilla extract
4½ cups all-purpose flour
1 teaspoon baking powder
1 teaspoon baking soda
1 teaspoon cream of tartar
Sifted powdered sugar

Combine butter and oil in a large mixing bowl; gradually add 1 cup sugar, beating well. Add eggs, beating well. Stir in vanilla.

Combine flour, baking powder, soda, and cream of tartar in a large mixing bowl; add to creamed mixture, stirring well.

Drop dough by teaspoonfuls 2 inches apart onto lightly greased cookie sheets. Bake at 325° for 12 to 15 minutes. Remove from cookie sheets, and cool on wire racks. Roll in powdered sugar. Yield: 6 dozen.

CINNAMON TEA CAKES

1 cup butter, softened
¾ cup sifted powdered sugar,
divided
½ teaspoon vanilla extract
1¾ cups all-purpose flour
1¼ teaspoons ground
cinnamon, divided

Cream butter in a large mixing bowl; gradually add ½ cup sugar, beating until light and fluffy. Stir in vanilla.

Sift together flour and 1 teaspoon cinnamon in a small mixing bowl; gradually add to creamed mixture, stirring well. Chill at least 1 hour.

Shape dough into 1-inch balls. Place 2 inches apart on ungreased cookie sheets. Bake at 350° for 12 to 15 minutes. Remove from cookie sheets, and cool on wire racks.

Combine remaining sugar and cinnamon, and sprinkle over tops of cookies while warm. Yield: 2 dozen.

Drop Tea Cakes and cut-out Butter Tea Cakes.

A Society of Patriotic Ladies, *1775 English caricature.*

EDENTON TEA PARTY CAKES

4 cups all-purpose flour
½ teaspoon salt
½ cup butter, softened
¼ cup lard, softened
1 teaspoon baking soda
1 tablespoon warm water
3 eggs
2 cups firmly packed
   brown sugar
1 teaspoon vanilla

Combine flour and salt in a large mixing bowl; cut in butter and lard with a pastry blender until mixture resembles coarse meal. Set aside.

Dissolve soda in water; stir well, and set aside.

Beat eggs in a large mixing bowl until foamy; add sugar and dissolved soda mixture, beating well. Stir in vanilla. Gradually add reserved flour mixture, stirring until well blended. Cover and chill thoroughly.

Roll dough to ¼-inch thickness on a lightly floured surface; cut with a 2-inch round cookie cutter. Place 2 inches apart on lightly greased cookie sheets. Bake at 400° for 7 minutes. Remove from cookie sheets, and cool on wire racks. Yield: about 6 dozen.

In 1774, fifty-one ladies of Edenton, North Carolina, in an unprecedented political activity, pledged not to drink tea. The English enjoyed the caricature (above) satirizing the ladies' gesture. But their "fixed intention and solemn determination" gained support when American newspapers printed an anonymous poem (below) that touched public sensibility.

A Lady's Adieu to Her Tea-Table
FAREWELL *the Tea-board with your gaudy attire,*
Ye cups and ye saucers that I did admire;
To my cream pot and tongs I now bid adieu;
That pleasure's all fled that I once found in you.
Farewell pretty chest that so lately did shine,
With hyson and congo and best double fine;
Many a sweet moment by you I have sat,
Hearing girls and old maids to tattle and chat;
And the spruce coxcomb laugh at nothing at all,
Only some silly work that might happen to fall.
No more shall my teapot so generous be
In filling the cups with this pernicious tea,
For I'll fill it with water and drink out the same,
Before I'll lose LIBERTY that dearest name,
Because I am taught (and believe it is fact)
That our ruin is aimed at in the late act,
Of imposing a duty on all foreign Teas,
Which detestable stuff we can quit when we please.
LIBERTY'S The Goddess that I do adore,
And I'll maintain her right until my last hour,
Before she shall part I will die in the cause,
For I'll never be govern'd by tyranny's laws.

Salem from the Southwest *was painted by Christian Daniel Welfare in 1824.*

NORTH CAROLINA TEA CAKES

½ cup shortening
1 cup sugar
2 eggs
1½ teaspoons vanilla extract
3¼ cups all-purpose flour
2 teaspoons baking powder
½ teaspoon salt
½ cup milk

Cream shortening in a large mixing bowl; gradually add sugar, beating well. Add eggs, one at a time, beating well after each addition. Stir in vanilla.

Combine flour, baking powder, and salt in a medium mixing bowl; add to creamed mixture alternately with milk, beginning and ending with flour mixture. Stir well after each addition.

Turn dough out onto a lightly floured surface. Roll to ⅛-inch thickness, and cut with a 2½-inch cookie cutter. Place 2 inches apart on lightly greased cookie sheets. Bake at 350° for 10 minutes or until lightly browned. Remove from cookie sheets, and cool on wire racks. Yield: 5 dozen.

MORAVIAN TEA CAKES

½ cup butter, softened
1 cup sugar
3 eggs
1½ teaspoons vanilla extract
½ teaspoon lemon extract
3 cups all-purpose flour
2 teaspoons baking powder
½ teaspoon salt
¾ teaspoon ground nutmeg

Cream butter in a large mixing bowl; gradually add sugar, beating well. Add eggs, one at a time, beating well after each addition. Stir in vanilla and lemon extract.

Sift together flour, baking powder, salt, and nutmeg in a medium mixing bowl. Gradually add to creamed mixture, stirring well after each addition.

Roll dough to ⅛-inch thickness on a heavily floured surface; cut dough with assorted cookie cutters. Place cookies 2 inches apart on lightly greased cookie sheets. Bake at 350° for 8 minutes. Remove from cookie sheets, and cool on wire racks. Yield: about 5½ dozen.

TEXAS TEA CAKES

1 cup butter, softened
1¼ cups sugar
3 eggs
½ teaspoon baking soda
2 tablespoons buttermilk
2 teaspoons vanilla extract
3¼ cups all-purpose flour
Dash of salt
1 cup chopped pecans
Additional sugar

Cream butter in a large mixing bowl; gradually add 1¼ cups sugar, beating well. Add eggs, one at a time, beating well after each addition.

Dissolve soda in buttermilk. Add buttermilk mixture and vanilla to creamed mixture, beating well. Combine flour, salt, and pecans; stir into creamed mixture. Chill.

Shape into 1-inch balls. Place 2 inches apart on lightly greased cookie sheets. Grease bottom of a glass; dip in sugar. Press each ball flat. Repeat procedure with remaining balls. Bake at 375° for 8 minutes or until lightly browned. Remove from cookie sheets, and cool on wire racks. Yield: 6 dozen.

MARY TELFAIR'S DERBY CAKES

7 cups all-purpose flour
2 cups butter
1 (10-ounce) package currants
2 cups sugar
1 egg, beaten
1 cup milk

Place flour in a large mixing bowl; cut in butter with a pastry blender until mixture resembles coarse meal. Stir in currants and sugar. Combine egg and milk; add to flour mixture. Mix well, and shape into a ball.

Roll dough to ⅛-inch thickness on a lightly floured surface. Cut into 3-inch circles. Place 2 inches apart on lightly greased cookie sheets. Bake at 350° for 12 to 15 minutes. Remove from cookie sheets, and cool on wire racks. Yield: about 5 dozen.

British architect William Jay's Regency style marks the handsome facade of the Telfair Mansion, built in 1818 for Alexander Telfair, son of Edward Telfair, one-time governor of Virginia and Revolutionary patriot. Alexander's sister, Mary, the last of the Telfairs, gave the property to the Georgia Historical Society in 1875. The Rotunda and Sculpture Gallery opened in 1886. Built for the Telfairs' original collections, the Museum's paintings and sculptures make it one of Georgia's most important shrines.

Telfair Academy of Arts and Sciences, legacy of a Savannah family. Mary Telfair (below).

MADELEINES

1¼ cups sifted cake flour
½ teaspoon baking powder
¼ teaspoon salt
3 eggs
1 teaspoon vanilla extract
⅔ cup sugar
2 teaspoons grated
  lemon rind
1 cup butter or margarine,
  melted and divided
Sifted powdered sugar
Chocolate Glaze

Sift together cake flour, baking powder, and salt in a small mixing bowl; set aside.

Beat eggs in a large mixing bowl until light and fluffy; add vanilla, beating well. Gradually add sugar, beating until volume of batter has increased 4 times.

Gradually fold in reserved flour mixture and grated lemon rind. Add ¾ cup melted butter, stirring until thoroughly blended. Set aside.

Brush madeleine pan with remaining ¼ cup melted butter; spoon reserved batter into each shell, filling three-fourths full. Bake at 350° for 12 minutes or until lightly browned.

Remove from madeleine pans, and cool completely on wire racks. Sprinkle each cookie with powdered sugar. Dip one-third of each cookie into Chocolate Glaze; place on waxed paper-lined cookie sheets, and refrigerate 2 hours. Store in airtight containers. Yield: 3 dozen.

Chocolate Glaze:

2 tablespoons strong
  coffee
2 tablespoons corn syrup
3 tablespoons butter or
  margarine
4 (1-ounce) squares
  semisweet chocolate,
  finely chopped

Combine coffee, syrup, and butter in a medium saucepan; bring to a boil, stirring constantly. Cook 30 seconds; remove from heat, and let stand an additional 30 seconds. Stir in chocolate with a wire whisk, beating until smooth. Yield: about 1 cup.

LADYFINGERS

Vegetable oil
All-purpose flour
3 eggs, separated
⅛ teaspoon salt
1 cup sifted powdered sugar,
  divided
1 teaspoon vanilla extract
⅔ cup sifted cake flour

Brush two cookie sheets lightly with oil; dust lightly with flour, and set aside.

Beat egg whites (at room temperature) and salt in a large mixing bowl until soft peaks form. Gradually add ⅓ cup sugar, 1 tablespoon at a time, beating until stiff peaks form. Set aside.

Combine egg yolks, ⅓ cup sugar, and vanilla in a small mixing bowl; beat at medium speed of an electric mixer 5 minutes or until thick and lemon colored. Gently fold yolk mixture into egg whites just until blended. Gradually fold in cake flour, ⅓ cup at a time, sifting flour over surface of egg mixture before folding.

Gently spoon mixture into a pastry bag fitted with a ½-inch round tip. Pipe mixture onto prepared cookie sheets in three ½-inch-long fingers, 2 inches apart. Sprinkle remaining ⅓ cup sugar lightly over ladyfingers, using a fine-meshed sieve. Bake at 350° for 8 minutes or until lightly browned. Yield: about 2 dozen.

Fashionable Georgia women at a tea party, c.1896.

DROP
AND BAKE

Drop cookies offer a quick fix to the occasional dilemma of "What can I serve? They'll be here in a couple of hours!" Throw the discussion open to the family, and you'll get a chorus of "chocolate chip," the cookie that's as popular now as benne seed cakes were a century ago. Our grandmothers taught us to like their old-time Hermits and Rocks. And we like to imitate their lovely frosted cookies, happy to take that extra step for the flavor and the looks of them. There's no sacrifice in taste, and drop cookies do save time.

Any lived-in kitchen can produce drop cookies: no chocolate chips or benne seeds? Look for oatmeal; everyone likes oatmeal cookies. Any nuts in the freezer? Dates or raisins? Coconut or a can of pineapple? Fruits, spices, pumpkin, carrots — drop cookies can materialize from a larder that looks nearly bare.

To Southerners who have served as Presidents of the United States their favorite cookies have been a taste of home while they served in Washington. Thomas Jefferson kept a decanter of wine and a plate of cakes in a cabinet in his bedroom. Included on the plate were sesame seed cakes (made from the African benne seed) and daintier cookies to be served up as bedtime snacks. Some were flavored with his own French import, vanilla.

Andrew Jackson, a South Carolinian, also served benne seed cakes to frequent (and frequently boisterous) gatherings at the White House. Martin Van Buren, the widower from New York who succeeded Jackson, was fortunate enough to have for a daughter-in-law and hostess a South Carolina girl, nee Angelica Singleton. It was through her influence that the benne seed cake once again became popular in the presidential inner circle.

Instances abound of presidents introducing favorite cookies to America, but it was Zachary Taylor's twenty-two-year-old daughter, Betty Bliss, acting as hostess when her mother was ill, who gave many Washington socialites their first taste of Maryland black pepper cakes.

Southern presidents from Washington to Carter, not to mention their constituents, have never "abjured their native victuals" as Tom Paine once accused Jefferson of doing.

Cookie jars are fun, but it's the contents that count. From front to rear: Double-Chocolate Cookies, Crunchy Oatmeal Cookies, and Carrot-Orange Cookies.

BAKE A BATCH

Prospect of Charles Town *by Bishop Roberts, c.1738.*

NUT DROP COOKIES

½ cup butter, softened
¾ cup sifted powdered sugar
2 egg yolks
1 tablespoon ice water
1 cup all-purpose flour
¼ teaspoon salt
½ teaspoon vanilla extract
Pecan halves

Cream butter in a medium mixing bowl; gradually add powdered sugar, beating until light and fluffy. Add egg yolks and water, beating until well blended.

Combine flour and salt in a small mixing bowl. Add to creamed mixture, beating well. Stir in vanilla.

Drop dough by teaspoonfuls 2 inches apart onto greased cookie sheets. Place a pecan half in center of each cookie; press down slightly. Bake at 375° for 8 minutes or until lightly browned. Remove from cookie sheets, and cool on wire racks. Yield: 3 dozen.

CHARLESTON VANILLA WAFERS

1½ tablespoons butter or margarine, softened
½ cup sugar
1 egg
½ teaspoon vanilla extract
¾ cup all-purpose flour
1 teaspoon baking powder
⅛ teaspoon salt
3 tablespoons milk

Cream butter in a medium mixing bowl; gradually add sugar, beating well. Add egg and vanilla; beat well.

Sift together flour, baking powder, and salt in a small mixing bowl; add to creamed mixture alternately with milk, beginning and ending with flour mixture. Stir well after each addition.

Drop dough by teaspoonfuls 2 inches apart onto greased cookie sheets. Bake at 350° for 6 to 8 minutes. Remove from cookie sheets, and cool on wire racks. Yield: 3 dozen.

BUTTERMILK DROP COOKIES

½ cup shortening
1 cup firmly packed brown sugar
1 egg
1 teaspoon vanilla extract
2¼ cups all-purpose flour
1 teaspoon baking powder
½ teaspoon baking soda
¼ teaspoon salt
¼ teaspoon ground nutmeg
½ cup buttermilk

Cream shortening in a large mixing bowl; gradually add sugar, beating well. Add egg and vanilla; beat well.

Sift together flour, baking powder, soda, salt, and nutmeg; add to creamed mixture alternately with buttermilk, beginning and ending with flour mixture. Stir well.

Drop by teaspoonfuls 2 inches apart onto greased cookie sheets. Bake at 375° for 8 to 10 minutes. Remove to wire racks to cool. Yield: 10 dozen.

THOMAS JEFFERSON'S BACHELOR BUTTONS

¾ cup butter or margarine,
  softened
1¾ cups sugar
2 eggs, beaten
1 teaspoon vanilla extract
3 cups all-purpose flour
2 teaspoons baking powder
½ teaspoon salt
Maraschino cherry halves,
  well drained

Cream butter and sugar in a large mixing bowl; add eggs and vanilla, beating well.

Sift together flour, baking powder, and salt in a medium mixing bowl; add to creamed mixture, mixing well.

Drop dough by teaspoonfuls 3 inches apart onto greased cookie sheets; press a cherry half in center of each cookie. Bake at 375° for 8 to 10 minutes. Remove from cookie sheets, and cool on wire racks. Yield: 4½ dozen.

LEMON DROP SUGAR COOKIES

1 cup shortening
2 cups sugar, divided
2 eggs
1 teaspoon lemon extract
1 teaspoon vanilla extract
2½ cups all-purpose flour
2 teaspoons baking powder
¼ teaspoon salt

Cream shortening in a large mixing bowl; gradually add 1½ cups sugar, beating well. Add eggs and flavorings; beat well.

Combine flour, baking powder, and salt in a small mixing bowl; gradually add to creamed mixture, stirring well.

Drop dough by heaping teaspoonfuls 3 inches apart onto greased cookie sheets. Gently press cookies with a fork to flatten. Sprinkle each cookie with remaining sugar. Bake at 375° for 10 minutes or until lightly browned. Remove from cookie sheets, and cool on wire racks. Yield: 8 dozen.

Contemporaries of Thomas Jefferson have written that he was a man of moderate eating habits, but that the food he did enjoy had to be of the finest quality. To have behaved otherwise would have been contradictory in the man whose mastery of so many arts is legendary. His well-documented fascination with matters culinary was congruent with his musical and architectural gifts, his experiments in botany, and his inventions of household and farming gadgetry. Bachelor Buttons would have fit right in with that plate of cakes in his bedroom cabinet with its touch-to-open doors.

Presidential snack: Thomas Jefferson's Bachelor Buttons.

FROSTED ORANGE COOKIES

1 cup shortening
2 cups sugar
2 eggs
4½ cups all-purpose flour
½ teaspoon baking powder
1 teaspoon baking soda
Dash of salt
1 cup buttermilk
Grated rind of 2 oranges,
    divided
⅔ cup orange juice, divided
1 (16-ounce) package
    powdered sugar, sifted

Cream shortening in a large mixing bowl; gradually add 2 cups sugar, beating well. Add eggs, one at a time, beating well after each addition.

Sift together flour, baking powder, soda, and salt in a small mixing bowl; add to creamed mixture alternately with buttermilk, beginning and ending with flour mixture. Beat well after each addition. Stir in half of grated rind and ⅓ cup orange juice, mixing well.

Drop dough by teaspoonfuls 2 inches apart onto greased cookie sheets. Bake at 375° for 10 minutes. Remove from cookie sheets, and cool on wire racks.

Combine remaining orange rind, juice, and powdered sugar in a medium mixing bowl, beating well; spread evenly over tops of cooled cookies. Yield: about 8½ dozen.

Illustration from Sunland's The Story of Dried Fruit.

PECAN HERMITS

¾ cup shortening
1½ cups firmly packed
    brown sugar
1 teaspoon ground cinnamon
½ teaspoon ground nutmeg
¼ teaspoon ground cloves
2 eggs, beaten
1 tablespoon milk
2½ cups all-purpose
    flour
½ teaspoon baking soda
¼ teaspoon salt
1 cup raisins, chopped
½ cup chopped pecans

Combine shortening, sugar, cinnamon, nutmeg, and cloves in a large mixing bowl, beating well. Add eggs and milk; beat until well blended.

Sift together flour, soda, and salt in a small mixing bowl. Add to sugar mixture, stirring well. Fold in raisins and pecans.

Drop dough by heaping teaspoonfuls 2 inches apart onto greased cookie sheets; flatten each cookie slightly using the back of a spoon. Bake at 350° for 12 minutes. Remove from cookie sheets, and cool on wire racks. Yield: 5 dozen.

HERMITS

½ cup firmly packed
    brown sugar
1 egg, beaten
½ teaspoon lemon extract
¼ teaspoon vanilla extract
½ cup raisins
1¼ cups bread flour
¼ teaspoon salt
½ teaspoon ground cinnamon
½ teaspoon ground allspice
¼ teaspoon ground nutmeg
¼ teaspoon ground cloves
½ cup shortening, melted
Additional raisins

Combine sugar and beaten egg in a large mixing bowl, beating well. Stir in flavorings and ½ cup raisins.

Sift together flour, salt, cinnamon, allspice, nutmeg, and cloves in a small mixing bowl; add to sugar mixture, stirring well. Stir in shortening.

Drop dough by teaspoonfuls 2 inches apart onto lightly greased cookie sheets; press a raisin in center of each cookie. Bake at 350° for 8 to 10 minutes. Remove from cookie sheets, and cool on wire racks. Yield: about 3½ dozen.

MARYLAND ROCKS

1 cup butter, softened
1½ cups sugar
3 eggs
2½ cups all-purpose flour
1 teaspoon baking soda
2 teaspoons ground
    cinnamon
1 cup raisins, chopped
1 cup black walnuts, coarsely
    chopped

Cream butter in a large mixing bowl; gradually add sugar, beating until light and fluffy. Add eggs, one at a time, beating well after each addition.

Combine flour, soda, and cinnamon. Add to creamed mixture, beating well. Stir in raisins and walnuts.

Drop by teaspoonfuls 2 inches apart onto greased cookie sheets. Bake at 350° for 8 to 10 minutes. Cool slightly on cookie sheets. Remove to wire racks to cool. Yield: about 9 dozen.

Hermits, from a vintage recipe, sit amid treasured collectio

ROCK COOKIES

1 cup butter or margarine, softened
1½ cups firmly packed brown sugar
3 eggs
3 tablespoons strong coffee
2½ cups all-purpose flour
1 teaspoon baking soda
1 tablespoon ground cinnamon
1 tablespoon ground allspice
1 cup raisins
1 cup chopped pecans

Cream butter in a large mixing bowl; gradually add sugar, beating until light and fluffy. Add eggs, one at a time, beating well after each addition. Add coffee, stirring well.

Combine flour, soda, cinnamon, and allspice in a large mixing bowl. Stir in raisins and pecans to coat well; add to creamed mixture.

Drop dough by heaping teaspoonfuls 2 inches apart onto greased cookie sheets. Bake at 350° for 8 minutes. Remove from cookie sheets, and cool on wire racks. Yield: about 5½ dozen.

SOUR CREAM ROCKS

½ teaspoon baking soda
⅓ cup commercial sour cream
¾ cup butter or margarine, softened
1¼ cups firmly packed brown sugar
3 eggs
2 cups all-purpose flour
1 teaspoon ground cinnamon
½ teaspoon ground nutmeg
1 cup raisins
1 cup pecan halves

Dissolve soda in sour cream; stir well. Set aside.

Cream butter in a large mixing bowl. Gradually add brown sugar; beat well. Add eggs, and beat well.

Combine flour, cinnamon, and nutmeg; stir in raisins and pecans to coat well. Add flour mixture and dissolved soda to creamed mixture, stirring until thoroughly blended.

Drop by teaspoonfuls 2 inches apart onto greased cookie sheets. Bake at 375° for 8 to 10 minutes. Remove from cookie sheets, and cool on wire racks. Yield: 8 dozen.

CRISP MOLASSES COOKIES

½ cup plus 2 tablespoons butter or margarine, melted
1 cup sugar
½ cup molasses
2 eggs
½ teaspoon vanilla extract
1¾ cups all-purpose flour
¼ teaspoon baking soda
¼ teaspoon salt
¼ teaspoon ground mace
2 cups chopped pecans

Combine butter, sugar, and molasses in a large mixing bowl, mixing well; add eggs and vanilla, beating well.

Sift together flour, soda, salt, and mace in a small mixing bowl; stir into butter mixture, ½ cup at a time, mixing well after each addition. Stir in pecans.

Drop dough by heaping teaspoonfuls 2 inches apart onto greased and floured cookie sheets. Bake at 350° for 8 minutes. Remove from cookie sheets, and cool on wire racks. Yield: about 5 dozen.

The New Orleans Coffee Company sold molasses under the Alligator label.

A baking class in progress, c.1900.

SPICY RAISIN-NUT COOKIES

1½ cups butter or margarine, softened
1 cup sugar
1 cup firmly packed brown sugar
2 eggs
1 teaspoon baking soda
1 cup buttermilk
4 cups all-purpose flour
½ teaspoon salt
¼ teaspoon ground cinnamon
¼ teaspoon ground nutmeg
¼ teaspoon ground ginger
1 cup chopped raisins
1 cup chopped pecans

Cream butter in a large mixing bowl; gradually add sugar, beating until light and fluffy. Add eggs, one at a time, beating well after each addition.

Dissolve soda in buttermilk; add to creamed mixture, beating until well blended.

Sift together flour, salt, cinnamon, nutmeg, and ginger; add to creamed mixture, stirring until well blended. Stir in raisins and pecans.

Drop dough by teaspoonfuls 4 inches apart onto greased cookie sheets. Bake at 425° for 6 to 8 minutes. Cool slightly on cookie sheets. Remove from cookie sheets, and cool completely on wire racks. Yield: about 10 dozen.

MARYLAND BLACK PEPPER COOKIES

2 eggs, separated
1 cup firmly packed brown sugar
1 cup all-purpose flour
¼ teaspoon baking powder
¼ teaspoon baking soda
¼ teaspoon salt
¼ teaspoon pepper
1 teaspoon ground cinnamon
½ teaspoon ground cloves
1 cup raisins
1 cup chopped walnuts

Beat egg whites (at room temperature) in a large mixing bowl until stiff peaks form. Beat egg yolks in a small mixing bowl until thick and lemon colored. Pour yolks into beaten egg whites, beating until thoroughly blended. Gradually add sugar, 2 tablespoons at a time, beating well.

Sift together flour, baking powder, soda, salt, pepper, cinnamon, and cloves in a medium mixing bowl. Gradually add to egg mixture. Add raisins and walnuts, stirring well.

Drop dough by heaping teaspoonfuls 2 inches apart onto lightly greased cookie sheets. Bake at 375° for 6 to 8 minutes. Cool slightly on cookie sheets. Remove from cookie sheets, and cool completely on wire racks. Yield: about 4½ dozen.

In 1709, a toll house was built midway between Boston and New Bedford at Whitman, Massachusetts. Coaches stopped to have refreshment, to change horses, and to pay a toll. In 1930, Mrs. Ruth Wakefield and her husband converted the house into an inn; it became famous for its food. One day Mrs. Wakefield chopped up a chocolate bar and added it to a colonial cookie recipe, assuming it would melt. It didn't; her customers loved the cookies. Nestlé introduced chocolate chips in 1939 and, with Mrs. Wakefield's permission, put her recipe on the package. Unfortunately, the inn burned down in early 1985.

ORIGINAL TOLL HOUSE® COOKIES

1 cup butter, softened
¾ cup sugar
¾ cup firmly packed brown sugar
2 eggs
1 teaspoon vanilla extract
2¼ cups all-purpose flour
1 teaspoon baking soda
1 teaspoon salt
1 (12-ounce) package semisweet chocolate morsels
1 cup chopped pecans

Cream butter in a large mixing bowl; gradually add sugar, beating until light and fluffy. Add eggs and vanilla; beat well.

Combine flour, soda, and salt in a small mixing bowl; gradually add to creamed mixture, stirring well. Stir in chocolate morsels and pecans.

Drop dough by heaping teaspoonfuls 2 inches apart onto ungreased cookie sheets. Bake at 375° for 8 minutes. Cool slightly on cookie sheets. Remove from cookie sheets, and cool completely on wire racks. Yield: 8½ dozen.

Both: Collection of Bonnie Slotnick

Ruth Wakefield (above) and her famous Toll House Inn (below), 1939.

Defense Cookies for a welcome gift package from home.

DEFENSE COOKIES

½ cup sugar
¼ cup firmly packed
  brown sugar
½ cup shortening
1 cup all-purpose flour
½ teaspoon baking soda
½ teaspoon salt
1 egg, beaten
1 teaspoon vanilla extract
1 (6-ounce) package
  semisweet chocolate
  morsels

Combine sugar in a medium mixing bowl. Cut in shortening with a pastry blender.

Sift together flour, soda, and salt in a small mixing bowl; add to sugar mixture, mixing well. Add egg and vanilla, stirring well. Stir in chocolate morsels.

Drop by teaspoonfuls 2 inches apart onto greased and floured cookie sheets. Bake at 350° for 8 to 10 minutes. Cool slightly on cookie sheets. Remove to wire racks to cool completely. Yield: about 3½ dozen.

BROWNIE DROP COOKIES

2 (4-ounce) packages sweet
  baking chocolate
1 tablespoon butter or
  margarine
2 eggs
¾ cup sugar
¼ cup all-purpose flour
¼ teaspoon baking powder
⅛ teaspoon salt
½ teaspoon vanilla extract
¾ cup chopped pecans

Combine chocolate and butter in top of a double boiler; bring water to a boil. Reduce heat to low; cook, stirring until chocolate and butter melt.

Beat eggs in a large mixing bowl until foamy; gradually add sugar, beating 5 minutes or until thickened. Add chocolate mixture, beating well.

Combine flour, baking powder, and salt in a small mixing bowl. Add to egg mixture, stirring until well blended. Fold in vanilla and pecans.

Drop dough by teaspoonfuls 2 inches apart onto greased cookie sheets. Bake at 350° for 10 minutes or until set. Cool slightly on cookie sheets. Remove to wire racks to cool completely. Yield: about 4 dozen.

39

CHOCOLATE CREAM COOKIES

½ cup butter or margarine,
  softened
½ cup shortening
1 (3-ounce) package cream
  cheese, softened
1½ cups sugar
1 egg
2 tablespoons milk
½ teaspoon vanilla extract
2 (1-ounce) squares
  unsweetened chocolate,
  melted
2¼ cups all-purpose flour
1½ teaspoons baking powder
½ teaspoon salt
½ cup chopped pecans

Cream butter, shortening, and cream cheese in a large mixing bowl; gradually add sugar, beating well. Add egg, milk, and vanilla; beat well. Stir in melted chocolate.

Sift together flour, baking powder, and salt in a small mixing bowl; gradually add to creamed mixture, mixing well after each addition. Stir in pecans.

Drop dough by teaspoonfuls 2 inches apart onto greased cookie sheets. Bake at 350° for 8 to 10 minutes. Cool slightly on cookie sheets. Remove from cookie sheets, and cool completely on wire racks. Yield: about 6 dozen.

CHOCOLATE ROCKS

¾ cup butter or margarine,
  softened
2 cups firmly packed
  brown sugar
2 eggs
4 (1-ounce) squares
  unsweetened chocolate,
  melted
2 teaspoons vanilla extract
2 cups all-purpose flour
2 teaspoons baking powder
1 teaspoon ground cinnamon
1 cup raisins
1 cup chopped pecans

Cream butter in a large mixing bowl; gradually add sugar, beating well. Add eggs, one at a time, beating well after each addition. Add chocolate and vanilla; beat well.

Sift together flour, baking powder, and cinnamon in a medium mixing bowl; add raisins and pecans, stirring to coat well. Add to creamed mixture.

Drop dough by teaspoonfuls 2 inches apart onto greased cookie sheets. Bake at 375° for 8 to 10 minutes. Remove from cookie sheets, and cool on wire racks. Yield: 11 dozen.

DOUBLE-CHOCOLATE COOKIES

4 (1-ounce) squares
  unsweetened chocolate,
  melted
1 cup butter or margarine,
  softened
2 cups sugar
4 eggs
2 teaspoons vanilla
  extract
¼ teaspoon salt
2 cups all-purpose flour
1 cup chopped pecans,
  toasted
1 (6-ounce) package
  semisweet chocolate
  morsels
Creamy Chocolate Filling

Cream butter in a large mixing bowl; gradually add sugar, beating well. Add melted chocolate, eggs, vanilla, and salt; mix well. Add flour to creamed mixture, stirring well. Stir in pecans and chocolate morsels.

Drop by heaping teaspoonfuls 2 inches apart onto greased cookie sheets. Bake at 350° for 10 minutes. Cool 1 minute on cookie sheets. Remove to wire racks to cool completely.

Spread bottom side of half the cookies with 1 to 2 teaspoons of Creamy Chocolate Filling. Top with remaining cookies to make a sandwich. Yield: 4½ dozen.

Creamy Chocolate Filling:

⅔ cup evaporated milk
½ cup water
2 teaspoons cornstarch
¼ cup sugar
2 tablespoons butter or
  margarine
⅛ teaspoon salt
1 (6-ounce) package
  semisweet chocolate
  morsels
1 teaspoon vanilla extract

Combine milk, water, and cornstarch in a small heavy saucepan, mixing well. Add sugar, butter, and salt. Cook over medium heat, stirring constantly, until thickened and smooth. Stir in chocolate morsels and vanilla. Chill thoroughly; stir before using. Yield: filling for 4½ dozen cookies.

The first Vallotton Dairy truck, Valdosta, Georgia, 1922.

PURE MILK AND CREAM
J.E. VALLOTTON
U.S. ACCREDITED HERD
PERMIT NO. 2   PHONE 1065

A promotion for W. H. Baker Chocolate and Cocoa, c.1900.

GOOD — AND GOOD FOR YOU

BRAN DROP COOKIES

½ cup butter or margarine,
  softened
¾ cup firmly packed
  brown sugar
2 eggs, beaten
1½ cups all-purpose flour
1½ teaspoons baking powder
½ teaspoon salt
½ teaspoon almond extract
½ teaspoon vanilla extract
1 cup wheat bran flakes
  cereal
½ cup chopped pecans
½ cup raisins

Cream butter in a large mixing bowl; gradually add sugar, beating until light and fluffy. Add eggs; mix well.

Sift together flour, baking powder, and salt; stir into creamed mixture. Stir in flavorings. Add remaining ingredients; mix well.

Drop dough by heaping teaspoonfuls 2 inches apart onto lightly greased cookie sheets. Bake at 400° for 8 minutes. Remove to wire racks to cool. Yield: about 4 dozen.

OATMEAL LACE COOKIES

½ cup sugar
1 egg, beaten
1½ teaspoons butter or
  margarine, melted
1¼ cups regular oats,
  uncooked
1¼ teaspoons baking powder
¼ teaspoon salt
½ teaspoon ground nutmeg
½ teaspoon vanilla extract

Gradually add sugar to egg in a medium mixing bowl, beating well. Add melted butter, mixing well. Combine oats, baking powder, salt, and nutmeg; add to egg mixture, beating well. Stir in vanilla.

Drop dough by teaspoonfuls 2 inches apart onto lightly greased cookie sheets. Bake at 350° for 6 minutes or until lightly browned. Remove from cookie sheets, and cool on wire racks. Yield: about 4 dozen.

A converted 1700s tavern: Raleigh Tavern Bakery, Williamsburg, Virginia.

OATMEAL-PECAN LACE COOKIES

1 cup butter or margarine,
  melted
3 cups firmly packed
  brown sugar
1 egg, beaten
1 teaspoon vanilla extract
2 cups regular oats, uncooked
1 cup chopped pecans

Combine butter and sugar in a large mixing bowl, mixing well. Add egg and vanilla, mixing well. Add oats and pecans, stirring well.

Drop by teaspoonfuls 3 inches apart onto aluminum foil-lined cookie sheets. Bake at 325° for 10 minutes. Cool on cookie sheets. Remove from aluminum foil; store in airtight containers. Yield: 9½ dozen.

RALEIGH TAVERN OATMEAL COOKIES

1 cup shortening
1 cup sugar
2 eggs
½ cup molasses
¼ cup milk
2 cups all-purpose flour
½ teaspoon baking soda
½ teaspoon salt
2 teaspoons ground
  cinnamon
1 teaspoon ground cloves
2 cups quick-cooking oats,
  uncooked

Cream shortening in a large mixing bowl; gradually add sugar, beating until light and fluffy. Add eggs, molasses, and milk; beat well.

Sift together flour, soda, salt, cinnamon, and cloves in a medium mixing bowl. Stir flour mixture into creamed mixture, stirring well. Add oats; stir well.

Drop dough by heaping tablespoonfuls 2 inches apart onto ungreased cookie sheets. Bake at 350° for 15 minutes. Cool slightly on cookie sheets. Remove to wire racks to cool. Yield: about 3 dozen.

The Colonial Williamsburg Foundation, Williamsburg, Virginia

Oatmeal Cookies. Clockwise from front plate: Lace, Raleigh Tavern, and Raisin (page 44)

OATMEAL-RAISIN COOKIES

½ cup butter
1 cup regular oats, uncooked
¼ cup milk
1 egg, beaten
1 cup all-purpose flour
½ cup sugar
½ teaspoon baking powder
½ teaspoon baking soda
¼ teaspoon salt
1 teaspoon ground cinnamon
1 teaspoon ground nutmeg
½ cup raisins
½ cup chopped pecans
1½ teaspoons vanilla extract

Melt butter in top of a double boiler over simmering water; add oats and milk, stirring well. Cover and cook 15 minutes. Remove from heat, and cool slightly; stir in egg.

Sift together flour, sugar, baking powder, soda, salt, cinnamon, and nutmeg in a small mixing bowl; add to oatmeal mixture, stirring well. Stir in raisins, pecans, and vanilla.

Drop dough by heaping teaspoonfuls 2 inches apart onto greased cookie sheets. Bake at 350° for 15 minutes. Cool slightly on cookie sheets. Remove to wire racks to cool completely. Yield: about 3½ dozen.

CHEWY OATMEAL COOKIES

½ cup butter, softened
½ cup lard, softened
1 cup sugar
1 cup firmly packed brown sugar
2 eggs
2 cups all-purpose flour
1 teaspoon baking powder
1 teaspoon baking soda
1 teaspoon salt
1½ cups quick-cooking oats, uncooked
½ cup chopped pecans
½ cup flaked coconut

Cream butter and lard in a large mixing bowl; gradually add sugar, beating well. Add eggs, and mix well.

Combine flour, baking powder, soda, and salt in a small mixing bowl; add to creamed mixture, stirring until well blended. Add oats, pecans, and coconut, mixing well.

Drop by heaping teaspoonfuls 2 inches apart onto lightly greased cookie sheets. Bake at 350° for 6 to 8 minutes. Remove from cookie sheets, and cool on wire racks. Yield: 10 dozen.

*Pre-Madison Avenue:
a trade card for Hornby's
3-Minute Oats, c.1890.*

CRUNCHY OATMEAL COOKIES

1 cup butter or margarine, softened
2 cups sugar
3 eggs
1 teaspoon vanilla extract
2 cups all-purpose flour
1 teaspoon baking soda
1 teaspoon salt
1½ cups regular oats, uncooked
1 cup chopped walnuts

Cream butter in a large mixing bowl; gradually add sugar, beating well. Add eggs and vanilla, beating well.

Sift together flour, soda, and salt in a small mixing bowl; stir into creamed mixture, mixing well. Stir in oats and walnuts.

Drop by teaspoonfuls 3 inches apart onto greased cookie sheets. Bake at 375° for 10 minutes or until golden brown. Remove from cookie sheets, and cool on wire racks. Yield: 10 dozen.

Note: One cup flaked coconut may be added to batter.

NO-BAKE CHOCOLATE-OATMEAL COOKIES

2 cups quick-cooking oats, uncooked
⅔ cup peanut butter
1 (3½-ounce) can flaked coconut
¼ cup cocoa
1 teaspoon vanilla extract
2 cups sugar
½ cup milk
¼ cup butter or margarine

Combine oats, peanut butter, coconut, cocoa, and vanilla, mixing well; set aside.

Combine sugar, milk, and butter in a small saucepan; bring to a boil. Cook 1 minute, stirring constantly. Pour over reserved oat mixture; quickly stir to mix well.

Immediately drop by heaping teaspoonfuls onto waxed paper-lined baking sheets; let cool. Carefully remove from waxed paper to serve. Yield: 4 dozen.

Brown Brothers

Looking like a modern-day automaton, this dandy machine stamped diamonds on walnuts, c.1920.

OATMEAL-CHOCOLATE CHIP COOKIES

3 cups regular oats, uncooked
¾ cup butter or margarine, softened
1 cup firmly packed brown sugar
½ cup sugar
1 egg
¼ cup water
2 teaspoons vanilla extract
1½ cups all-purpose flour
½ teaspoon baking soda
½ teaspoon salt
1 (6-ounce) package semisweet chocolate morsels

Spread oats on ungreased cookie sheet. Bake at 350° for 10 minutes. Remove from oven, and set aside.

Cream butter in a large mixing bowl; gradually add sugar, beating well. Add egg, water, and vanilla; beat well.

Sift together flour, soda, and salt in a medium mixing bowl; add reserved oats and chocolate morsels, stirring to coat well. Stir flour mixture into creamed mixture.

Drop batter by heaping teaspoonfuls 2 inches apart onto greased cookie sheets. Bake at 350° for 10 minutes or until lightly browned. Cool slightly on cookie sheets. Remove to wire racks to cool completely. Yield: 7 dozen.

Oats were not mentioned in the Bible, nor did they have their beginnings in the Mediterranean area. Obscure as to origin, they were first noted in northern Europe during the Bronze Age, at the same time horses began to be used as draft animals. If a spirited horse seems to be "feeling his oats," he has a long history of doing so. Oats are a leading crop in Britain and America, still important as animal feed. But from those early Britishers, we inherited a liking for oats as cereal too. And oatmeal cookies, soft or crisp, are just plain wonderful.

Juliette Gordon Low Cookies and Rolled Benne Wafers.

JULIETTE GORDON LOW COOKIES

¾ cup butter or margarine, softened
1½ cups firmly packed brown sugar
2 eggs
1¼ cups all-purpose flour
¼ teaspoon baking powder
½ cup sesame seeds, toasted
1 teaspoon vanilla extract

Cream butter in a medium mixing bowl; gradually add sugar, beating well. Add eggs, one at a time, beating well after each addition.

Combine flour and baking powder in a small mixing bowl; add to creamed mixture, beating well. Stir in sesame seeds and vanilla.

Drop dough by teaspoonfuls 2 inches apart onto waxed paper-lined cookie sheets. Bake at 325° for 12 to 15 minutes. Cool completely on cookie sheets. Remove from waxed paper, and store cookies in airtight containers. Yield: about 10 dozen.

Juliette Gordon Low, founder of the Girl Scouts of the U.S.A., was born in Savannah, Georgia, in 1860 and died there in 1927. Though incurably deaf, she was a gifted artist and writer, well educated, and widely traveled. When she married William Mackay Low, she moved to England. Widowed in 1905 and without children of her own, she found her calling when she returned home in 1912 and, with 18 girls, founded what is now the Girl Scouts. Her Savannah home is the Girl Scout National Center.

ROLLED BENNE WAFERS

½ cup butter
½ cup dark corn syrup
¼ cup firmly packed brown sugar
¾ teaspoon vanilla extract
¾ cup all-purpose flour
Dash of salt
½ cup sesame seeds, toasted

Combine butter, corn syrup, sugar, and vanilla in a medium saucepan; cook over medium heat, stirring frequently, until butter melts. Add flour and salt; stir until well blended. Bring to a boil, stirring constantly. Remove from heat, and stir in sesame seeds. Place pan in a bowl of hot water.

Drop batter by teaspoonfuls onto greased cookie sheets. Bake at 375° for 5 minutes.

Remove from oven, and let stand for 1 minute. Shape each wafer around the buttered handle of a wooden spoon. Slide off, and place on a wire rack to cool completely. (Bake only 5 wafers at a time because they harden quickly after baking.) Repeat procedure with remaining batter. Store wafers in airtight containers. Yield: 3 dozen.

*An 1880s portrait of
Juliette Gordon Low
(above). Girl Scout Cookies
carried in baskets (right)
prior to the 1934 boxes.
Banner held by Scouts
and their founder (below).*

WITH FRUITS AND NUTS

APPLESAUCE COOKIES

½ cup butter or margarine,
  softened
1 cup sugar
1 egg, beaten
1 teaspoon baking soda
1 cup applesauce
2 cups all-purpose flour
½ teaspoon salt
½ teaspoon ground cinnamon
½ teaspoon ground nutmeg
1 cup raisins
½ cup chopped pecans

Cream butter in a large mixing bowl; gradually add sugar, beating well. Add egg; mix well.

Combine soda and applesauce in a small mixing bowl. Stir into creamed mixture.

Sift together flour, salt, cinnamon, and nutmeg in a small mixing bowl; stir into creamed mixture. Fold in raisins and pecans.

Drop dough by heaping teaspoonfuls 3 inches apart onto greased cookie sheets. Bake at 375° for 10 to 12 minutes. Remove from cookie sheets, and cool on wire racks. Yield: about 5 dozen.

APPLE-MOLASSES DROP COOKIES

½ cup shortening
½ cup sugar
1 egg
1 cup molasses
3 tablespoons lemon juice,
  divided
3½ cups all-purpose flour
2 teaspoons baking soda
⅛ teaspoon salt
1 teaspoon ground cinnamon
¾ teaspoon ground cloves
½ teaspoon ground ginger
1 cup boiling water
1½ cups finely chopped
  peeled apple
2¼ cups sifted powdered
  sugar
3 tablespoons butter or
  margarine, softened
Grated lemon rind

Cream shortening in a large mixing bowl; gradually add ½ cup sugar, beating until light and fluffy. Add egg; beat well. Add molasses and 1 tablespoon lemon juice, stirring well.

Sift together flour, soda, salt, cinnamon, cloves, and ginger in a medium mixing bowl; add to creamed mixture alternately with boiling water, beginning and ending with flour mixture. Stir well after each addition. Fold in chopped apple. Chill dough 1 hour.

Drop dough by teaspoonfuls 2 inches apart onto greased cookie sheets. Bake at 350° for 10 minutes. Remove from cookie sheets, and cool on wire racks.

Combine powdered sugar, butter, and remaining lemon juice in a small mixing bowl; beat at medium speed of an electric mixer until smooth. Spread evenly over tops of cooled cookies. Sprinkle each with grated lemon rind. Yield: 11 dozen.

This monument to the apple-growing industry in Habersham County is located in Cornelia, Georgia.

Fruit has a delicious effect on cookies, as proved by Banana Cake Cookies (front) and Apricot Jewels.

BANANA CAKE COOKIES

½ cup shortening
1 cup firmly packed
   brown sugar
2 eggs
1 cup mashed ripe banana
2 cups all-purpose flour
2 teaspoons baking powder
½ teaspoon baking soda
½ teaspoon salt
½ teaspoon ground cinnamon
½ teaspoon ground cloves
½ cup chopped pecans
Powdered Sugar Icing

Cream shortening in a large mixing bowl; gradually add sugar, beating well. Add eggs and banana; beat well.

Sift together flour, baking powder, soda, salt, cinnamon, and cloves in a small mixing bowl; add to creamed mixture, stirring well. Stir in pecans.

Drop dough by tablespoonfuls 2 inches apart onto greased cookie sheets. Bake at 350° for 12 minutes. Remove from cookie sheets, and cool on wire racks. Spread tops of cooled cookies with Powdered Sugar Icing. Yield: about 3½ dozen.

Powdered Sugar Icing:

3 cups sifted powdered sugar
1 tablespoon butter or
   margarine, melted
¾ teaspoon vanilla extract
3 to 6 tablespoons milk

Combine first 3 ingredients in a small mixing bowl; add milk to desired consistency. Beat until smooth. Yield: about 1½ cups.

APRICOT JEWELS

1¼ cups all-purpose flour
¼ cup sugar
¾ teaspoon baking powder
⅛ teaspoon salt
½ cup butter or margarine,
   softened
1 (3-ounce) package cream
   cheese, softened
½ cup flaked coconut
½ cup apricot preserves

Sift together flour, sugar, baking powder, and salt in a large mixing bowl. Cut in butter and cream cheese with a pastry blender until mixture resembles coarse meal. Stir in coconut and apricot preserves.

Drop dough by teaspoonfuls 2 inches apart onto ungreased cookie sheets. Bake at 350° for 10 to 12 minutes. Remove from cookie sheets, and cool on wire racks. Yield: about 4 dozen.

Fig orchard in Houston, Texas, just months after planting, c.1913.

DATE DROP COOKIES

⅔ cup shortening
1 cup sugar
2 eggs
1 teaspoon baking soda
¼ cup warm water
2 cups all-purpose flour
¼ teaspoon salt
¾ teaspoon ground cinnamon
¼ teaspoon ground cloves
2 (8-ounce) packages chopped dates
1 cup chopped pecans

Cream shortening in a large mixing bowl; gradually add sugar, beating until light and fluffy. Add eggs, one at a time, beating well after each addition. Dissolve soda in water; stir into creamed mixture.

Sift together flour, salt, cinnamon, and cloves in a medium mixing bowl; add dates and pecans, stirring to coat well. Add to creamed mixture, stirring until thoroughly blended.

Drop dough by heaping teaspoonfuls 2 inches apart onto lightly greased cookie sheets. Bake at 350° for 12 to 14 minutes. Remove from cookie sheets, and cool on wire racks. Yield: about 7½ dozen.

STUFFED DATE COOKIES

2 (8-ounce) packages pitted dates
2 cups pecan halves
¼ cup butter or margarine, softened
¾ cup firmly packed brown sugar
1 egg
1¼ cups all-purpose flour
½ teaspoon baking powder
½ teaspoon baking soda
¼ teaspoon salt
½ cup commercial sour cream

Stuff each date with a pecan half, and set aside.

Cream butter in a medium mixing bowl; gradually add sugar, beating well. Add egg; beat well.

Sift together flour, baking powder, soda, and salt; add to creamed mixture alternately with sour cream, beginning and ending with flour mixture. Fold in prepared dates.

Drop dough by heaping teaspoonfuls 2 inches apart onto greased cookie sheets, allowing 1 date per cookie. Bake at 375° for 6 minutes or until lightly browned. Remove from cookie sheets, and cool on wire racks. Yield: 6½ dozen.

FIG DROP COOKIES

1 cup dried figs
½ cup shortening
¾ cup sugar
1 egg
½ cup molasses
¾ teaspoon vanilla extract
2 cups all-purpose flour
1 teaspoon baking soda
¼ teaspoon salt
½ teaspoon ground cinnamon
½ teaspoon ground ginger
½ cup chopped pecans

Combine figs and enough warm water to cover in a small mixing bowl; let stand 30 minutes. Drain well, and chop figs. Set aside.

Cream shortening in a large mixing bowl; gradually add sugar, beating until light and fluffy. Add egg, molasses, and vanilla; beat well.

Sift together flour, soda, salt, cinnamon, and ginger in a medium mixing bowl; add reserved figs and pecans, stirring to coat well. Stir flour mixture into creamed mixture; mix well.

Drop dough by teaspoonfuls 2 inches apart onto greased cookie sheets. Bake at 350° for 10 minutes or until lightly browned. Cool slightly on cookie sheets, and remove to wire racks. Yield: about 8 dozen.

CARROT-ORANGE COOKIES

¾ cup shortening
¾ cup sugar
1 cup mashed, cooked carrots
1 egg
1 teaspoon vanilla extract
¾ teaspoon orange extract
2 cups all-purpose flour
2 teaspoons baking powder
¼ teaspoon salt
½ cup raisins
½ cup chopped pecans

Cream shortening in a large mixing bowl; gradually add sugar, beating until light and fluffy. Add carrots, egg, vanilla, and orange extract; beat well.

Combine flour, baking powder, and salt; add to creamed mixture, stirring well. Stir in raisins and pecans.

Drop dough by heaping teaspoonfuls 2 inches apart onto greased cookie sheets. Bake at 350° for 12 to 15 minutes. Remove from cookie sheets, and cool on wire racks. Yield: about 7 dozen.

PERSIMMON COOKIES

2 tablespoons butter or margarine, softened
1 cup sugar
1½ cups all-purpose flour
1½ teaspoons baking powder
2 teaspoons baking soda
1 teaspoon ground cinnamon
¼ teaspoon ground cloves
¼ teaspoon ground allspice
¼ teaspoon ground nutmeg
1 cup persimmon pulp, pureed
1 cup chopped walnuts
½ cup raisins
½ cup finely chopped dates
1½ teaspoons grated orange rind
1 teaspoon vanilla extract

Cream butter in a medium mixing bowl; gradually add sugar, beating well.

Combine flour, baking powder, soda, cinnamon, cloves, allspice, and nutmeg in a small mixing bowl. Add to creamed mixture alternately with persimmon puree, beginning and ending with flour mixture; beat well after each addition. Stir in remaining ingredients.

Drop dough by heaping teaspoonfuls 2 inches apart onto lightly greased cookie sheets. Bake at 375° for 8 minutes or until lightly browned. Remove from cookie sheets, and cool on wire racks. Yield: about 5 dozen.

Bemused and world-weary, "An orange-man" hesitates in his stroll to be sketched for an 1887 trade card.

PUMPKIN SPICE COOKIES

½ cup shortening
1⅓ cups sugar
2 eggs
1 cup mashed, cooked
    pumpkin
1 teaspoon vanilla extract
½ teaspoon lemon extract
1 teaspoon grated lemon rind
2½ cups all-purpose flour
1 tablespoon baking powder
1 teaspoon salt
1 teaspoon ground cinnamon
1 teaspoon ground nutmeg
½ teaspoon ground allspice
¼ teaspoon ground ginger
1 cup raisins
½ cup chopped pecans
Lemon Butter Cream Frosting
    (optional)

Cream shortening in a large mixing bowl; gradually add sugar, beating well. Add eggs, one at a time, beating well after each addition. Stir in pumpkin, vanilla, lemon extract, and grated lemon rind.

Combine flour, baking powder, salt, and spices in a medium mixing bowl; stir well. Gradually add to creamed mixture, stirring well. Stir in raisins and pecans.

Drop batter by teaspoonfuls 2 inches apart onto greased cookie sheets. Bake at 375° for 12 minutes or until lightly browned. Remove from cookie sheets, and cool on wire racks. Frost with Lemon Butter Cream Frosting, if desired. Yield: 7 dozen.

Lemon Butter Cream Frosting:

¼ cup butter, softened
2¼ cups sifted powdered
    sugar, divided
3 tablespoons half-and-half
½ teaspoon grated lemon rind

Cream butter in a medium mixing bowl; gradually add 1 cup powdered sugar, beating well with electric mixer. Add remaining powdered sugar alternately with half-and-half, beating until smooth enough to spread. Add lemon rind, and beat well. Yield: frosting for 7 dozen cookies.

PINEAPPLE COOKIES

3 cups all-purpose flour
1 teaspoon baking powder
1 teaspoon baking soda
½ teaspoon salt
1 cup shortening
1 (8¼-ounce) can crushed
    pineapple, undrained
1½ cups firmly packed
    brown sugar
1 egg, beaten

Sift together flour, baking powder, soda, and salt in a large mixing bowl; cut in shortening with a pastry blender until mixture resembles coarse meal.

Combine pineapple, sugar, and egg in a small mixing bowl; stir well. Add to flour mixture, stirring well.

Drop by teaspoonfuls 2 inches apart onto greased cookie sheets. Bake at 325° for 10 to 12 minutes or until lightly browned. Remove from cookie sheets, and cool on wire racks. Yield: 10½ dozen.

GREEK ALMOND COOKIES

¾ cup butter or margarine,
    softened
¾ cup sugar
1 egg
½ teaspoon almond extract
¾ cup ground, blanched
    almonds
1½ cups all-purpose flour
¼ teaspoon salt

Cream butter in a medium mixing bowl; gradually add sugar, beating until light and fluffy. Add egg and almond extract; beat well. Stir in almonds, mixing well.

Combine flour and salt in a small mixing bowl; add to creamed mixture, stirring well.

Drop dough by heaping teaspoonfuls 2 inches apart onto greased cookie sheets. Bake at 375° for 8 to 10 minutes. Remove from cookie sheets, and cool on wire racks. Yield: 4 dozen.

Greek engagement party with Almond Cookies, Houston, 1938.

Houston Metropolitan Research Center

Pumpkin Spice Cookies, with and without frosting.

FLORENTINES

¼ cup butter or margarine
1 cup sugar
¾ cup whipping cream
3 tablespoons sifted cake
    flour
1¼ cups ground almonds
1 teaspoon orange extract
1 teaspoon vanilla extract
2 cups sliced almonds

Combine butter, sugar, and whipping cream in a medium saucepan. Bring to a boil, stirring constantly. Stir in flour and ground almonds; mix well. Remove from heat; stir in orange extract, vanilla, and sliced almonds.

Drop dough by teaspoonfuls 3 inches apart onto aluminum foil-lined cookie sheets. Bake at 350° for 8 to 10 minutes. Let cool completely on cookie sheets; peel off aluminum foil. Store cookies in airtight containers. Yield: about 9 dozen.

PECAN CRISPIES

2 egg whites
1 cup firmly packed
    brown sugar
¼ cup all-purpose flour
2 cups pecan halves

Beat egg whites (at room temperature) in a medium mixing bowl until stiff peaks form. Gradually sprinkle sugar over beaten whites; continue to beat until well blended. Fold in flour and pecans.

Drop dough by teaspoonfuls 2 inches apart onto greased and floured cookie sheets. Bake at 300° for 20 to 25 minutes. Remove from cookie sheets, and cool on wire racks. Yield: about 4 dozen.

A playful ambush in a 1916 advertisement for Post Toasties, "The Perfect Corn Flakes."

PECAN LACE COOKIES

2 eggs, beaten
1 cup plus 2½ tablespoons
    firmly packed brown sugar
½ cup all-purpose flour
¼ teaspoon baking powder
Dash of salt
½ teaspoon vanilla extract
2 cups chopped pecans

Combine eggs and sugar in a large mixing bowl, stirring well.

Combine flour, baking powder, and salt in a small mixing bowl; add to egg mixture. Mix well. Stir in vanilla and pecans.

Drop dough by heaping teaspoonfuls 3 inches apart onto aluminum foil-lined cookie sheets. Bake at 350° for 8 minutes. Let cool completely on cookie sheets; peel off aluminum foil. Store cookies in airtight containers. Yield: 5 dozen.

THE HOLD-UP

NEW POST TOASTIES

Crisp—Delicious—The Perfect Corn Flakes

GERMAN PECAN BRITTLES

1 cup shortening
1 cup sugar
1 cup firmly packed
  brown sugar
2 eggs
2 cups all-purpose flour
1 teaspoon baking powder
1 teaspoon baking soda
1 teaspoon salt
1 cup corn flakes cereal,
  crushed
1 cup chopped pecans
1 teaspoon vanilla extract

Cream shortening in a large mixing bowl; gradually add sugar, beating well. Add eggs, one at a time, beating well after each addition.

Sift together flour, baking powder, soda, and salt in a medium mixing bowl; add cereal and pecans, stirring to coat well. Stir flour mixture and vanilla into creamed mixture, mixing well.

Drop dough by teaspoonfuls 2 inches apart onto greased and floured cookie sheets. Bake at 325° for 10 to 12 minutes. Remove from cookie sheets, and cool on wire racks. Yield: 11 dozen.

German Pecan Brittles: the name is recommendation enough.

Nearly all the English walnuts consumed in America come from California. They originated in Persia, but the black walnut is native to the eastern United States; Indians were eating them some 3,000 years ago. The English nut is so bland that it sometimes serves as "crunch"; the black walnut, by contrast, is so potent that many object. It is often used in equal portions with English walnuts to diminish the strong flavor. Black walnut products should not be stored with other flavors; their odor will permeate the rest.

WALNUT WAFERS

2 eggs
1⅓ cups firmly packed
  brown sugar
¼ cup plus 1 tablespoon
  all-purpose flour
⅛ teaspoon baking powder
⅛ teaspoon salt
1 teaspoon vanilla extract
1 cup chopped walnuts

Beat eggs in a medium mixing bowl until thick and tripled in volume; gradually add sugar, beating well. Stir in flour, baking powder, salt, and vanilla. Stir in walnuts.

Drop dough by teaspoonfuls 2 inches apart onto parchment- or aluminum foil-lined cookie sheets. Bake at 375° for 6 minutes or until lightly browned. Cool completely on cookie sheets, and store in airtight containers. Yield: about 5 dozen.

ROLL TO CUT, CHILL TO SET

When George Washington retired to Mount Vernon after his term as President, it was his hope to spend quiet times with his wife, look after his farm, and otherwise rest up after so many years of service to the nation. The public followed him, of course, but Martha Washington tried hard to make his life simple and happy. One of their little institutions was afternoon refreshments of cookies and hot mulled chocolate.

After a long horseback ride, Washington liked nothing better than Martha's sugar cakes, rolled thin and "cut rather large"; nothing was mentioned about how they were cut out. Her chocolate cakes, however, were rolled and cut out with a knife into strips an inch wide, baked, and stacked on a plate log-cabin style. Improvisation was rife; the cakes could have been cut with a household glass, as in the days of Hannah Glasse, or even with a tin box lid.

But it is entirely possible that Mrs. Washington had cake cutters or "moulds." Household inventories from eighteenth-century Virginia list various moulds. Ironmongers, pewterers and tinsmiths had all added fancy cutters to their wares, and serious cooks invested in them. By 1824, Mary Randolph's *The Virginia Housewife* could end "Shrewsbury Cakes" and "Plebeian Ginger Bread" recipes with "Roll thin and cut it with tin shapes." And jumbles were soon being "cut out with a cake cutter," probably a doughnut shape, to make the traditional ring form. Cookie cutters reached some sort of peak in 1913 when Walter Baker & Co., Ltd. published a recipe for "Turkey Trots," requiring a turkey-shaped cutter. The baked cookie was to have the words *Turkey Trot* written on it in icing. It was named, naturally, for the ragtime dance craze that lasted through World War I.

The Frigidaire Corporation published the first recipe for "chill-slice-and-bake" cookies in 1929. Three variations are given, along with instructions for forming pinwheels. Yet, the concept seems so simple: hadn't someone ever used a cool back porch instead of a refrigerator? Still, we can readily imagine the joy with which the home baker welcomed that new piece of equipment into her kitchen.

These are easy cookies; you'll need bushels of them for children (they'll help make them) and other aficionados.

Diamond-shaped Molasses Cookies and Oma's Sugar Cookies are as much at home in the bedroom of the Terrill Home in Fredericksburg, Texas, as they were when the antiques were new.

COOKIE-CUTTER MAGIC

WALDEN'S RIDGE TOLL HOUSE SUGAR COOKIES

½ cup butter, softened
1 cup sugar
1 egg
1 teaspoon vanilla
    extract
1 teaspoon baking soda
¼ cup buttermilk
3 cups all-purpose flour

Cream butter in a large mixing bowl; gradually add sugar, beating well. Add egg, and beat well. Stir in vanilla.

Dissolve soda in buttermilk; add to creamed mixture, stirring well. Gradually add flour; mix well. Chill 1 hour.

Divide dough in half, keeping one half chilled until ready to use. Roll to ¼-inch thickness on a well-floured surface, and cut with a floured 2½-inch round cutter.

Place 1 inch apart on lightly greased cookie sheets. Bake at 350° for 8 to 10 minutes. Remove from cookie sheets, and cool on wire racks. Repeat procedure with remaining dough. Yield: about 4 dozen.

DECORATOR SUGAR COOKIES

3 cups all-purpose flour
2 teaspoons baking powder
¾ teaspoon baking soda
½ teaspoon ground
    nutmeg
1 cup shortening
2 eggs, beaten
1 cup sugar
¼ cup milk
1 teaspoon vanilla extract
Powdered Sugar Glaze

Combine flour, baking powder, soda, and nutmeg in a large mixing bowl; cut in shortening with a pastry blender until mixture resembles coarse crumbs.

Combine eggs, sugar, milk, and vanilla in a small mixing bowl; mix well, and pour into crumb mixture. Stir with a fork until moistened. Shape into a ball. Chill 1 hour.

Divide dough in half, keeping one half chilled until ready to use. Roll to ⅛-inch thickness on a lightly floured surface; cut with assorted cookie cutters.

Place on lightly greased cookie sheets; bake at 375° for 5 minutes or until edges are lightly browned. Remove from cookie sheets, and cool on wire racks. Repeat procedure with remaining dough. Decorate as desired with Powdered Sugar Glaze. Yield: about 5 dozen.

Powdered Sugar Glaze:

2 cups sifted powdered sugar
3 to 4 tablespoons milk
1 teaspoon vanilla extract
Paste food coloring

Combine sugar, milk, and vanilla; stir until smooth. Color small amounts of glaze with food coloring to decorate as desired. Yield: about 1½ cups.

Gordon Wetmore

Walden's Ridge Toll House, *a watercolor by Gordon Wetmore.*

In 1852, Josiah N. Anderson built a toll road across Walden's Ridge, a few miles out of Chattanooga. Even when rebuilt later, it was called *W Road* because the switch-back curves looked like a *W* from the top. Anderson's Pike gave access from the Sequatchie Valley to the new Western and Atlantic Railroad between Chattanooga and Atlanta. Six years later, James C. Conner moved to Walden's Ridge and built a large cabin of oak and poplar logs. Travelers could spend the night at Conner's Toll House or simply enjoy a snack of cookies and buttermilk and go on across the mountain. The last surviving Conner died at the old Toll House in 1974. The restored cabin now houses a collection of artifacts related to Cumberland Mountain culture.

OMA'S SUGAR COOKIES

¾ cup butter or margarine, softened
2 cups sugar
2 eggs
¼ cup milk
1 teaspoon almond extract
4 cups all-purpose flour
1 tablespoon baking powder
¼ teaspoon ground nutmeg
Additional sugar

Cream butter in a large mixing bowl; gradually add 2 cups sugar, beating well. Add eggs, one at a time, beating well after each addition; add milk, beating well. Stir in almond extract.

Sift together flour, baking powder, and nutmeg in a medium mixing bowl. Gradually add flour mixture to creamed mixture, stirring well after each addition. Cover and chill several hours or overnight.

Divide dough in half, keeping one half chilled until ready to use. Roll to 1/16-inch thickness on a well-floured surface, and cut with assorted floured cookie cutters.

Place 1 inch apart on lightly greased cookie sheets. Sprinkle with additional sugar. Bake at 350° for 10 to 12 minutes. Remove from cookie sheets, and cool on wire racks. Repeat procedure with remaining dough. Yield: about 9 dozen.

LEMON COOKIES

1 cup butter or margarine, softened
2 cups sugar
2 eggs
Grated rind and juice of 1 large lemon
1 teaspoon lemon extract
¼ teaspoon baking soda
½ cup milk
5½ cups all-purpose flour
2 tablespoons baking powder

Cream butter in a large mixing bowl; gradually add sugar, beating well. Add eggs, one at a time, beating well after each addition. Stir in lemon rind and juice and lemon extract.

Dissolve soda in milk, stirring well. Sift together flour and baking powder in a medium mixing bowl; gradually add to creamed mixture alternately with milk mixture, beginning and ending with flour mixture. Stir well after each addition. Cover and chill at least 1 hour.

Divide dough in half, keeping one half chilled until ready to use. Turn half of dough out onto a well-floured surface, working additional flour into dough, if necessary. Roll to ⅛-inch thickness, and cut with assorted cookie cutters.

Place on greased cookie sheets, and bake at 325° for 15 minutes. Cool slightly on cookie sheets. Remove from cookie sheets, and cool completely on wire racks. Repeat procedure with remaining dough. Yield: about 9 dozen.

A 1940s promotion for Dixie Crystals, a product of the Savannah Sugar Refinery.

Shrewsbury Cakes taste like great-grandmother's, no matter what shape we cut them.

MOLASSES COOKIES

1 cup shortening
2 cups sugar
2 teaspoons baking soda
2 cups dark molasses
¾ cup water
¼ cup rum
7 cups all-purpose flour
1 tablespoon salt
1 tablespoon ground ginger
1 teaspoon ground nutmeg
1 teaspoon ground cloves
½ teaspoon ground
  allspice
Pecan halves

Cream shortening in a large mixing bowl; gradually add sugar, beating well.

Dissolve soda in molasses in a small mixing bowl; stir until well blended, and set aside. Combine water and rum, stirring well; set aside.

Sift together flour, salt, and spices in a large mixing bowl; gradually add to creamed mixture alternately with reserved molasses and rum mixtures, beginning and ending with flour mixture, stirring well after each addition. Divide dough in half; wrap each half in waxed paper, and chill overnight.

Work with one half of dough, keeping remaining dough chilled until ready to use. Roll to ⅛-inch thickness on a well-floured surface. Cut with a diamond-shaped cutter. Place on lightly greased cookie sheets, and firmly press a pecan half in center of each cookie.

Bake at 350° for 10 minutes or until lightly browned and crisp. Remove from cookie sheets, and cool on wire racks. Repeat procedure with remaining dough and pecans. Yield: about 10 dozen.

SAND DOLLARS

½ cup butter or margarine,
  softened
1¼ cups sugar, divided
1 egg
1 teaspoon vanilla extract
2 cups all-purpose flour
1½ teaspoons baking powder
1 egg white, lightly beaten
1 teaspoon ground cinnamon

Cream butter in a medium mixing bowl; gradually add 1 cup sugar, beating well. Add 1 egg and vanilla; beat well.

Sift together flour and baking powder. Gradually add to creamed mixture; stir well. Cover and chill 1 hour.

Divide dough in half, keeping one half chilled. Roll to ⅛-inch thickness on a well-floured surface, and cut with a 2½-inch round cutter.

Place on greased cookie sheets; brush with egg white. Combine remaining sugar and cinnamon in a small mixing bowl; sprinkle half of sugar mixture over cookies.

Bake at 350° for 10 minutes or until lightly browned. Cool slightly on cookie sheets, and remove to wire racks. Repeat procedure with remaining dough, egg whites, and sugar mixture. Yield: about 3½ dozen.

SHREWSBURY CAKES

½ cup butter or margarine,
  softened
½ cup shortening
1 cup sugar
3 eggs
4½ cups all-purpose flour
1½ teaspoons baking powder
1½ teaspoons ground
  cinnamon
1½ teaspoons ground nutmeg

Combine butter and shortening in a large mixing bowl; beat at medium speed of an electric mixer just until blended. Gradually add sugar, beating until light and fluffy. Add eggs, one at a time, beating well.

Sift together flour, baking powder, cinnamon, and nutmeg in a medium mixing bowl; gradually add to creamed mixture, stirring well after each addition. Cover and chill 1 hour.

Divide dough in half, keeping one half chilled until ready to use. Roll to ⅛-inch thickness on a well-floured surface, and cut with a 2½-inch round cutter.

Place on lightly greased cookie sheets, and bake at 375° for 8 minutes. Cool slightly on cookie sheets. Remove to wire racks to cool completely. Repeat procedure with remaining dough. Yield: 3½ dozen.

Lady Managers representing the World's Columbian Exposition donated autographed recipes to a cookery book as a means of helping less fortunate women attend the 1893 World's Fair. Susan G. Cooke, Secretary of the Lady Managers, compiled the recipes along with her own cookie recipe (right). A souvenir card from the World's Fair (below) features a chocolate marvel.

SUSAN G. COOKE'S EXPOSITION COOKIES

1 cup butter or margarine, softened
1½ cups sugar
3 eggs
3 cups all-purpose flour
1 teaspoon baking soda
1 teaspoon ground cinnamon
1 teaspoon ground allspice
1 teaspoon ground cloves
1 cup chopped raisins

Cream butter in a large mixing bowl; gradually add sugar, beating until light and fluffy. Add eggs; beat well.

Sift together flour, soda, and spices in a medium mixing bowl; add to creamed mixture, stirring well. Stir in raisins. Cover and refrigerate overnight.

Roll to ¼-inch thickness on a lightly floured surface; cut with a 2½-inch round cutter. Place 2 inches apart on lightly greased cookie sheets; bake at 350° for 8 to 10 minutes. Remove from cookie sheets, and cool on wire racks. Yield: about 5 dozen.

BITTER CHOCOLATE COOKIES

¾ cup butter, softened
1 cup sugar
⅛ teaspoon salt
1 egg
4 (1-ounce) squares unsweetened chocolate, melted
1 teaspoon vanilla extract
1¾ cups all-purpose flour

Cream butter in a medium mixing bowl; gradually add sugar and salt, beating until light and fluffy. Add egg, beating well.

Stir melted chocolate and vanilla into creamed mixture. Stir in flour. Chill 1 hour.

Roll to ¼-inch thickness on a lightly floured surface. Cut with a 2-inch round cutter. Place 2 inches apart on lightly greased cookie sheets; bake at 425° for 6 to 8 minutes. Cool slightly on cookie sheets. Remove to wire racks to cool completely. Yield: about 4 dozen.

CHOCOLATE SANDWICH COOKIES

½ cup butter or margarine,
   softened
1¼ cups sugar
3 (1-ounce) squares
   unsweetened chocolate,
   melted
1 teaspoon vanilla extract
2 eggs
2½ cups all-purpose flour
1½ teaspoons baking powder
½ teaspoon baking soda
½ teaspoon salt
Filling (recipe follows)

Cream butter in a large mixing bowl; gradually add sugar, beating well. Add melted chocolate and vanilla; beat well. Add eggs, one at a time, beating well after each addition.

Combine flour, baking powder, soda, and salt in a small mixing bowl. Stir flour mixture into creamed mixture. Divide dough in half; wrap in waxed paper, and chill 1 hour.

Roll half of dough to ⅛-inch thickness on a lightly floured surface; keep remaining dough chilled until ready to use. Cut with a 2½-inch fluted or round cookie cutter. Place 2 inches apart on ungreased cookie sheets. Bake at 350° for 8 to 10 minutes. Remove from cookie sheets, and cool on wire racks.

Repeat procedure with remaining dough, cutting out center of each cookie with a ½-inch round cookie cutter before baking.

Prepare filling. Spread solid cookies evenly with filling. Top with remaining cookies to make sandwiches, pressing down slightly to fill cut-outs on tops of cookies. Yield: 1½ dozen.

Filling:

⅔ cup shortening
¼ teaspoon salt
½ teaspoon vanilla extract
⅓ cup water
1 (16-ounce) package
   powdered sugar, sifted

Combine shortening, salt, and vanilla in a medium mixing bowl; beat at medium speed of an electric mixer until blended. Add small amounts of water alternately with sugar, beating at low speed until blended. Beat an additional 8 minutes at medium speed until smooth. Yield: about 2⅓ cups.

Note: Frosting may be stored at room temperature or in refrigerator for several days.

Southerners coveted chocolates from San Francisco's Ghirardelli Chocolate Co. Here, the wrapping and packing room, c.1920.

SOUR CREAM COOKIES

1 cup butter or margarine,
   softened
2 cups sugar
3 eggs
½ cup commercial sour
   cream
1 teaspoon baking soda
4 cups all-purpose flour

Cream butter in a large mixing bowl; gradually add sugar, beating well. Add eggs, beating well. Add sour cream and soda; beat well. Stir in flour. Cover and chill overnight.

Roll half of dough to ¼-inch thickness on a floured surface; keep remaining dough chilled. Cut with floured 2-inch cutters into desired shapes.

Place 2 inches apart on lightly greased cookie sheets; bake at 450° for 5 minutes or until lightly browned. Remove from cookie sheets, and cool on wire racks. Yield: about 5 dozen.

CREAM CHEESE THUMBPRINT COOKIES

1 cup butter, softened
2 (3-ounce) packages cream
  cheese, softened
2 cups all-purpose flour
2 tablespoons sugar
2 teaspoons baking powder
Strawberry jam
Powdered sugar (optional)

Combine butter and cream cheese in a large mixing bowl, beating until light and fluffy. Add flour, 2 tablespoons sugar, and baking powder, stirring until well blended.

Roll dough to ¼-inch thickness on a lightly floured surface. Cut with a 1½-inch fluted or round cutter. Place 2 inches apart on ungreased cookie sheets. Press center of each cookie slightly with thumb. Fill center of each cookie with ¼ teaspoon jam.

Bake at 350° for 10 to 12 minutes. Remove from cookie sheets, and place on wire racks to cool. Sift powdered sugar over tops of cookies, if desired. Yield: about 7 dozen.

CREAM CHEESE HORNS

½ cup butter, softened
1 (3-ounce) package cream
  cheese, softened
1½ cups sifted cake flour
2 tablespoons sugar
½ teaspoon salt
1 tablespoon whipping cream
½ teaspoon vanilla extract
Pineapple jelly or raspberry
  jelly
½ cup finely chopped pecans
2 egg whites, lightly beaten
Finely chopped pistachio nuts

Combine butter and cream cheese in a large mixing bowl, beating well.

Combine flour, sugar, and salt in a small mixing bowl. Add to creamed mixture, stirring well. Stir in whipping cream and vanilla; mix well. Cover and refrigerate overnight.

Roll to ⅛-inch thickness on a lightly floured surface; cut with a 2-inch round cutter. Place ¼ teaspoon jelly in center of cookie; sprinkle with pecans. Fold opposite edges over filling and pinch together, forming a cornucopia. Brush open end of

cornucopia with egg whites; dip in pistachio nuts. Repeat procedure with remaining cookies, egg whites, and nuts.

Place 2 inches apart on lightly greased cookie sheets; bake at 325° for 15 minutes. Remove from cookie sheets, and cool on wire racks. Yield: about 4 dozen.

LINZER COOKIES

1½ cups butter, softened
1 cup sugar
2 eggs
1 teaspoon vanilla extract
14 ounces blanched whole
  almonds, finely ground
3⅓ cups sifted cake flour
1 teaspoon baking powder
1 teaspoon ground
  cinnamon
Raspberry jam
Powdered sugar

Cream butter in a large mixing bowl; gradually add 1 cup sugar, beating until light and fluffy. Add eggs and vanilla, beating well; stir in ground almonds, mixing well.

Sift together flour, baking powder, and cinnamon in a small mixing bowl; gradually add to creamed mixture, stirring well after each addition. Cover and refrigerate overnight.

Roll one-fourth of dough to ¼-inch thickness between two pieces of waxed paper, keeping remaining dough chilled until ready to use.

Cut with a fluted 2-inch round cutter; place half of cookies on lightly greased cookie sheets. Cut centers from remaining cookies, using a ¾-inch round cutter; place on lightly greased cookie sheets. Bake at 350° for 10 to 12 minutes. Remove from cookie sheets, and cool on wire racks. Repeat procedure with remaining dough.

Spread a small amount of jam on the bottom of each solid cookie. Top with remaining cookies to make sandwiches. Sift powdered sugar over tops of cookies. Fill cut-outs with jam. Store in airtight containers. Yield: about 2½ dozen.

Cream Cheese Horns, when you want a truly exquisite sweet.

ITALIAN PILLOWS

1 cup shortening
1 cup sugar
2 teaspoons vanilla extract
¼ teaspoon salt
4 eggs
4 hard-cooked egg yolks
3¾ cups all-purpose flour
½ cup whipping cream
1 (10-ounce) jar orange
  marmalade, divided
1 egg white, unbeaten

Cream shortening in a large mixing bowl; gradually add sugar, beating until light and fluffy. Add vanilla and salt; beat well. Add 4 eggs, one at a time, beating well after each addition. Press hard-cooked egg yolks through a sieve into creamed mixture, stirring well.

Add flour to creamed mixture alternately with whipping cream, beginning and ending with flour. Stir well after each addition. Cover and chill several hours or overnight.

Work with one-fourth of dough at a time, keeping remaining dough chilled until ready to use. Roll to ¼-inch thickness on a well-floured surface, and cut into 2-inch squares. Place ¼ teaspoon orange marmalade in center of each square. Fold dough into a triangle, and press edges together with a fork. Brush tops with egg white.

Place 2 inches apart on lightly greased cookie sheets. Bake at 350° for 15 minutes or until lightly browned. Remove to wire racks to cool. Repeat procedure with remaining dough, marmalade, and egg whites. Yield: about 8 dozen.

Grecian Date Rolls (front) with whole dates wrapped in dough and coated with pecans. Italian Pillows conceal orange marmalade.

GRECIAN DATE ROLLS

¾ cup butter or margarine,
  softened
1 cup sugar, divided
1 egg yolk
3 cups all-purpose
  flour
½ cup milk
2 (8-ounce) packages
  pitted dates
1 cup chopped
  pecans
2 egg whites, lightly beaten

Cream butter in a large mixing bowl; gradually add ½ cup sugar, beating until light and fluffy. Add egg yolk; beat well. Gradually add flour to creamed mixture alternately with milk, beginning and ending with flour, beating well after each addition. Chill 1 hour.

Divide dough into 3 equal portions. Roll each portion to ⅛-inch thickness between two sheets of waxed paper. Cut into 2-inch squares. Place 1 date in center of each square; fold and press dough around date.

Combine pecans and remaining sugar in a small mixing bowl; stir well. Dip cookies in egg whites (at room temperature); roll in pecan mixture.

Place 2 inches apart on greased cookie sheets. Bake at 350° for 20 minutes or until lightly browned. Remove from cookie sheets, and cool on wire racks. Store in airtight containers. Yield: 6½ dozen.

APRICOT TURNOVERS

1 (6-ounce) package dried
  apricots
1¼ cups water
2 cups sugar, divided
½ cup butter or margarine,
  softened
2 cups all-purpose flour
1 (16-ounce) carton creamed
  cottage cheese
2 egg whites, lightly beaten
1 cup ground pecans

Combine apricots and water in a heavy saucepan; cook over medium heat 30 minutes or until tender. Drain; place apricots in a medium mixing bowl, and mash until smooth. Stir in ¾ cup sugar; chill overnight.

Cream butter; gradually stir in flour and cottage cheese. Shape mixture into 1-inch balls, and chill overnight.

Combine remaining sugar and pecans in a small mixing bowl; set aside.

Roll balls to a 3-inch diameter on a lightly floured surface. Place 1 teaspoon chilled apricot mixture in center; fold over, and pinch edges together. Dip into egg whites; roll in reserved pecan mixture, and place on greased cookie sheets. Bake at 375° for 12 to 14 minutes. Remove from cookie sheets, and cool on wire racks. Yield: about 4 dozen.

Note: Cottage cheese balls and apricot mixture may be refrigerated up to 2 weeks to prepare turnovers as needed.

A novice ready for cookie-making, 1890.

Brown Brothers

Most of an almond-hulling crew hard at work, c.1890.

ALMOND ICEBOX COOKIES

2 cups butter or margarine, softened
2 cups sugar
4 cups all-purpose flour
2 teaspoons baking powder
1 teaspoon vanilla extract
1 egg white, lightly beaten
Finely chopped almonds

Cream butter in a large mixing bowl; gradually add sugar, beating until light and fluffy.

Combine flour and baking powder in a medium mixing bowl; mix well. Add flour mixture and vanilla to creamed mixture, stirring well.

Divide dough in half; shape each half into a roll, 1½ inches in diameter. Wrap each roll in waxed paper, and refrigerate 2 hours.

Cut rolls into ¼-inch slices. Place on lightly greased cookie sheets. Brush lightly with egg white; sprinkle with almonds. Bake at 425° for 10 minutes or until lightly browned. Remove to wire racks to cool. Yield: about 7½ dozen.

SHAKER VANILLA COOKIES

½ cup butter or margarine, softened
¾ cup sugar
1 egg
1¼ teaspoons vanilla extract
1½ cups all-purpose flour
1 teaspoon baking powder
¼ teaspoon salt

Cream butter in a large mixing bowl; gradually add sugar, beating until light and fluffy. Add egg and vanilla, beating until well blended.

Sift together flour, baking powder, and salt in a medium mixing bowl; add to creamed mixture, mixing well.

Shape dough into a long roll, 1½ inches in diameter; wrap roll in waxed paper, and refrigerate 2 hours or until thoroughly chilled.

Cut into ¼-inch slices. Place 3 inches apart on lightly greased cookie sheets; bake at 400° for 8 minutes. Remove from cookie sheets, and cool on wire racks. Yield: about 3 dozen.

VANILLA NUT ICEBOX COOKIES

1 cup shortening
1 cup sugar
¼ cup firmly packed brown sugar
1 egg, beaten
2 teaspoons vanilla extract
1 cup chopped pecans
2 cups all-purpose flour
1½ teaspoons baking powder
¼ teaspoon salt

Cream shortening in a large mixing bowl; gradually add sugar, beating until light and fluffy. Add egg and vanilla; beat well. Stir in pecans.

Combine flour, baking powder, and salt in a medium mixing bowl; gradually add to creamed mixture, stirring well.

Divide dough in half; shape each half into a roll, 2 inches in diameter. Wrap each in waxed paper; chill until firm.

Cut into ¼-inch slices. Place 1 inch apart on ungreased cookie sheets. Bake at 425° for 5 minutes. Remove from cookie sheets, and cool on wire racks. Yield: about 5 dozen.

SWEDISH COOKIES

½ cup butter, softened
½ cup sifted powdered sugar
1 teaspoon vanilla extract
1 cup all-purpose flour
½ cup ground pecans

Cream butter in a medium mixing bowl; gradually add sugar, beating until light and fluffy. Stir in vanilla. Gradually add flour and pecans, stirring just until blended.

Shape dough into a roll, 2 inches in diameter; wrap each roll in waxed paper, and chill several hours until firm.

Cut into ¼-inch slices. Slice circles in half; place halves 1 inch apart on ungreased cookie sheets. Bake at 375° for 5 minutes. Remove from cookie sheets, and cool on wire racks. Yield: about 5 dozen.

BUTTERSCOTCH COOKIES

1½ cups butter, softened
2 cups firmly packed
   brown sugar
2 eggs
3 cups all-purpose flour
2 teaspoons baking powder

Cream butter in a large mixing bowl; gradually add sugar, beating until light and fluffy. Add eggs, one at a time, beating well after each addition. Stir in flour and baking powder, mixing well.

Divide dough in half; shape each half into a roll, 2 inches in diameter. Wrap in waxed paper, and chill overnight or until firm.

Cut into ¼-inch slices; place 2 inches apart on ungreased cookie sheets. Bake at 375° for 8 minutes or until lightly browned. Remove from cookie sheets, and cool on wire racks. Yield: about 7 dozen.

Pinwheel cookies appeal to man, woman, and child. Front to rear: Date (page 70), Chocolate (page 68), and Butterscotch.

BUTTERSCOTCH PINWHEELS

½ cup shortening, divided
¼ cup firmly packed
   brown sugar
1 egg
¾ cup butterscotch morsels,
   melted
1 teaspoon vanilla extract,
   divided
2 cups all-purpose flour,
   divided
¼ teaspoon baking soda
½ teaspoon salt, divided
½ cup sugar
1 egg
¼ teaspoon baking powder
1 (1-ounce) square
   unsweetened chocolate,
   melted

Cream ¼ cup shortening in a medium mixing bowl; gradually add ¼ cup brown sugar, beating until light and fluffy. Add 1 egg, beating well. Stir in melted butterscotch morsels and ½ teaspoon vanilla.

Sift together 1 cup flour, soda, and ¼ teaspoon salt in a small mixing bowl; add to creamed mixture, stirring until well blended.

Roll to a 10- x 7-inch rectangle between two sheets of waxed paper; set aside.

Repeat mixing and rolling procedure with remaining ingredients, substituting ½ cup granulated sugar for brown sugar, baking powder for soda, and chocolate for butterscotch.

Remove waxed paper from tops of dough, and invert chocolate rectangle directly on top of butterscotch rectangle. Remove remaining waxed paper. Roll up jellyroll fashion, beginning with long side; wrap in waxed paper. Chill at least 1 hour.

Cut into ¼-inch slices. Place 2 inches apart on lightly greased cookie sheets. Bake at 375° for 6 minutes or until lightly browned. Remove from cookie sheets, and cool on wire racks. Yield: about 5½ dozen.

DUTCH CHEESE WAFERS

½ cup butter, softened
1 (3-ounce) package cream
  cheese, softened
½ cup sugar
1 cup all-purpose flour
½ cup finely chopped dried
  apricots or peaches

Combine butter and cream cheese in a medium mixing bowl. Gradually add sugar, beating until light and fluffy. Stir in flour and apricots. Mix well.

Shape into a roll, 1-inch in diameter. Wrap in waxed paper, and chill 3 hours or until firm.

Cut into ¼-inch slices; place 1 inch apart on ungreased cookie sheets. Bake at 350° for 8 to 10 minutes. Remove from cookie sheets, and cool on wire racks. Yield: about 7 dozen.

CHOCOLATE ICEBOX COOKIES

1 cup butter or margarine,
  softened
¾ cup light corn syrup
½ cup sugar
3 cups all-purpose flour
¾ cup cocoa
½ teaspoon baking powder
¼ teaspoon salt
1 cup chopped pecans

Cream butter in a large mixing bowl; gradually add corn syrup and sugar, beating until smooth. Combine remaining ingredients in a medium mixing bowl, stirring well; gradually add to creamed mixture, stirring well.

Shape dough into two rolls, 2 inches in diameter; wrap in waxed paper, and chill.

Cut into ⅛-inch slices. Place 1 inch apart on ungreased cookie sheets. Bake at 400° for 5 minutes. Remove from cookie sheets, and cool on wire racks. Yield: about 10 dozen.

Trade card for Bensdorp's Royal Dutch Cocoa, c.1890.

Collection of Kit Barry, Brattleboro, Vermont

CHOCOLATE-WALNUT REFRIGERATOR COOKIES

1¼ cups butter or margarine,
  softened
1 cup sugar
2 eggs
4 (1-ounce) squares
  semisweet chocolate,
  melted
1 teaspoon vanilla extract
3½ cups all-purpose flour
1 tablespoon baking powder
½ teaspoon salt
2 cups chopped walnuts

Cream butter in a large mixing bowl; gradually add sugar, beating until light and fluffy. Add eggs, one at a time, beating well after each addition. Add melted chocolate and vanilla, beating until well blended.

Combine flour, baking powder, and salt; add to creamed mixture, stirring well. Stir in walnuts.

Divide dough in half; shape each half into a roll, 2 inches in diameter. Wrap in waxed paper, and chill overnight or until firm.

Cut dough into ⅛-inch slices; place 2 inches apart on ungreased cookie sheets. Bake at 350° for 8 to 10 minutes. Remove from cookie sheets, and cool on wire racks. Yield: about 13 dozen.

CHOCOLATE PINWHEEL COOKIES

½ cup butter or margarine,
  softened
½ cup sugar
3 tablespoons milk
1 egg yolk, beaten
½ teaspoon vanilla extract
1½ cups all-purpose flour
1½ teaspoons baking powder
⅛ teaspoon salt
1 (1-ounce) square
  unsweetened chocolate,
  melted

Cream butter in a medium mixing bowl; gradually add sugar, beating until light and fluffy. Add milk, egg yolk, and vanilla, stirring well.

Sift together flour, baking powder, and salt; add to creamed mixture, stirring until well blended.

Divide dough in half; set one half aside. Add melted chocolate to remaining dough; stir until well blended. Chill.

Roll light half of dough to a 14- x 6-inch rectangle on waxed paper; set aside. Repeat procedure with chocolate dough. Gently place chocolate rectangle directly on top of light rectangle; remove waxed paper. Roll up jellyroll fashion, beginning at long side; wrap in waxed paper, and chill 1 hour.

Cut into ¼-inch slices. Place 2 inches apart on greased cookie sheets. Bake at 375° for 8 to 10 minutes. Cool slightly on cookie sheets, and remove to wire racks. Yield: about 5 dozen.

CITRUS WAFERS

1 cup butter or margarine, softened
1 cup sugar
2 eggs
1½ teaspoons vanilla extract
3 cups all-purpose flour
1 teaspoon salt
1 tablespoon grated orange rind
Orange food coloring
1½ teaspoons grated lemon rind
Yellow food coloring
1½ teaspoons grated lime rind
Green food coloring
Tinted granulated sugar (optional)

Cream butter in a large mixing bowl; gradually add sugar, beating until light and fluffy. Add eggs and vanilla; mix well. Combine flour and salt; add to creamed mixture, mixing well.

Divide dough in half; set one half aside. Add orange rind and orange food coloring to half of dough, mixing until well blended. Divide orange dough in half; wrap in waxed paper, and chill.

Divide remaining dough in half. Add lemon rind and yellow food coloring to one half, mixing well; wrap in waxed paper, and chill. Add lime rind and green food coloring to remaining dough, mixing well; wrap in waxed paper, and chill.

Shape each chilled portion of dough into two long rolls, 1 inch in diameter; wrap each roll in waxed paper, and chill an additional 30 minutes.

Place two orange rolls, one lemon roll, and one lime roll together lengthwise, alternating colors. Press rolls together firmly to form 1 roll; wrap in waxed paper, and chill. Repeat procedure with remaining dough.

Cut into ¼-inch slices, and place 2 inches apart on greased cookie sheets. Sprinkle with tinted sugar, if desired. Bake at 350° for 8 minutes. Remove from cookie sheets, and cool completely on wire racks. Yield: 4 dozen.

Early twentieth-century postcard showing Florida oranges being harvested.

PICKING ORANGES IN FLORIDA—F102

Special Collections, University of South Florida Library

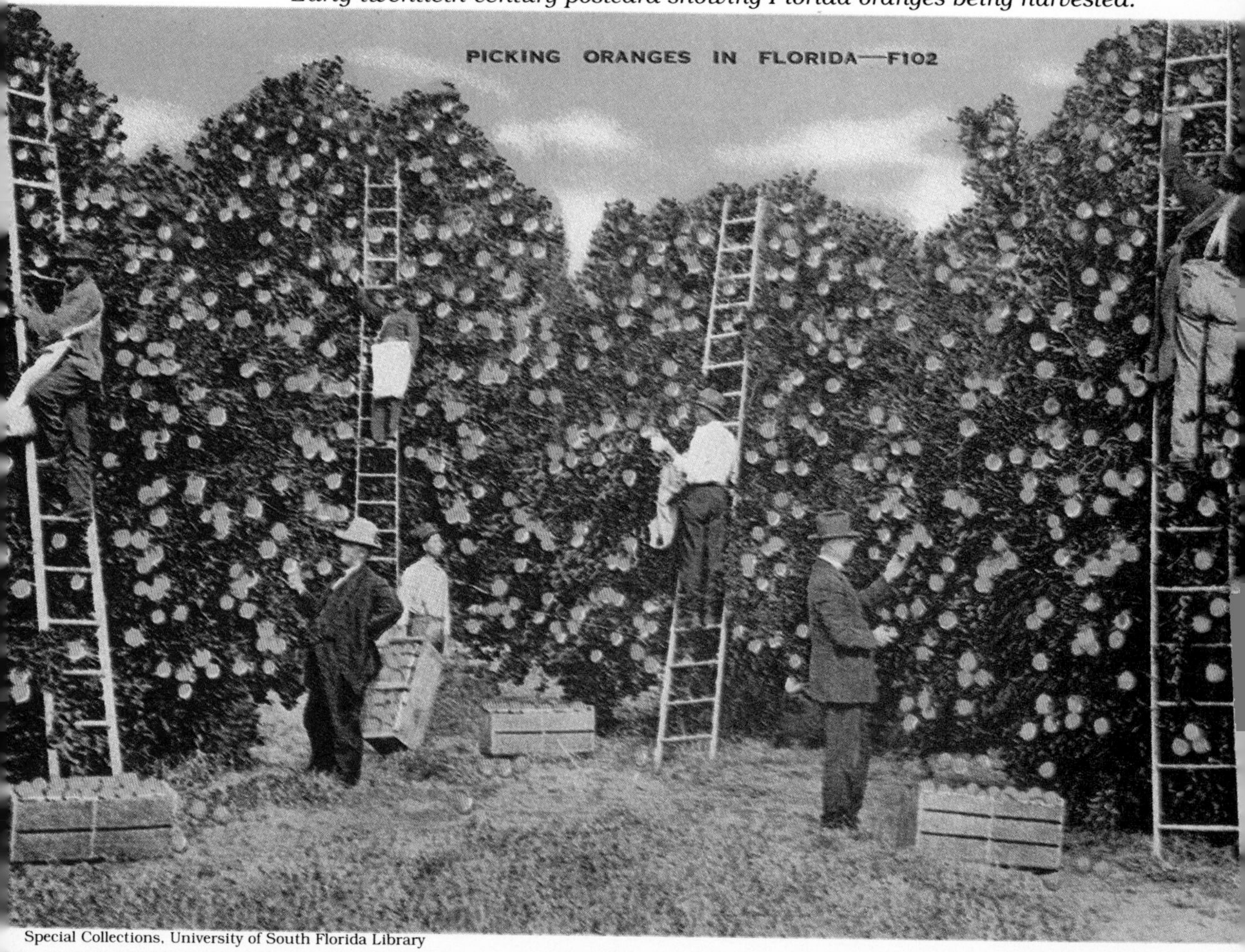

COCONUT ICEBOX COOKIES

3 eggs, lightly beaten
1 cup sugar
½ cup firmly packed
  brown sugar
1½ cups shortening, melted
4 cups grated coconut
5½ cups sifted cake flour
1 tablespoon baking powder
¼ teaspoon salt

Combine eggs, sugar, shortening, and coconut in a large mixing bowl; mix well.

Sift together flour, baking powder, and salt. Add to egg mixture, stirring well.

Press dough into a waxed paper-lined 8-inch square baking pan; cover and refrigerate overnight.

Turn dough out of pan, and remove waxed paper. Slice dough in half, forming two 8- x 4-inch rectangles. Cut each portion crosswise into ¼-inch slices. Place on ungreased cookie sheets; bake at 400° for 10 minutes or until lightly browned. Remove from cookie sheets, and cool on wire racks. Yield: about 5 dozen.

Back cover of Baker's Coconut Recipes *booklet, c.1925.*

All the Real Flavor and Tenderness of the Freshly Opened Nut

BAKER'S Southern-Style COCONUT

Collection of Bonnie Slotnick

DATE PINWHEEL COOKIES

1 (8-ounce) package pitted
  dates
½ cup water
¼ cup sugar
½ cup butter or margarine,
  softened
1 cup firmly packed
  brown sugar
1 egg
2 cups all-purpose flour
½ teaspoon baking soda
¼ teaspoon salt
½ teaspoon ground cinnamon

Combine dates, water, and ¼ cup sugar in a medium saucepan. Bring to a boil. Reduce heat, and simmer 5 minutes, stirring constantly. Remove from heat, and set aside to cool completely.

Cream butter in a large mixing bowl; gradually add brown sugar, beating well. Add egg; beat well. Combine flour, soda, salt, and cinnamon. Stir into creamed mixture. Cover and chill at least 1 hour.

Roll to a 16- x 10-inch rectangle on waxed paper; spread evenly with reserved date filling. Roll up jellyroll fashion; pinch ends to seal. Wrap in waxed paper, and chill overnight.

Cut into ¼-inch slices. Place 3 inches apart on ungreased cookie sheets. Bake at 375° for 8 minutes or until lightly browned. Remove from cookie sheets, and cool on wire racks. Yield: about 4½ dozen.

To add variety to a cookie tray, just make pinwheels! Two colors, as in chocolate and vanilla, are easiest, but the possibilities are larger than that: spread dough with a date or other fruit mixture of your own devising. Try apricots or a favorite jam, nuts if you like, so long as the consistency is manageable.

Peanut Butter Refrigerator Cookies are easily chilled, sliced, and baked.

HONEY COOKIES

½ cup butter or margarine,
  softened
½ cup sugar
1 egg, lightly beaten
½ cup honey
2 cups all-purpose flour
2 teaspoons baking powder
½ teaspoon salt
1 cup chopped pecans

Cream butter in a large mixing bowl; gradually add sugar, beating until light and fluffy.

Combine egg and honey, mixing well. Set aside.

Sift together flour, baking powder, and salt in a medium mixing bowl. Add to creamed mixture, stirring well. Stir in reserved egg mixture and pecans. Mix well.

Shape into a roll, 1½ inches in diameter. Wrap in waxed paper, and refrigerate overnight.

Cut into ¼-inch slices. Place on lightly greased cookie sheets, and bake at 375° for 10 to 15 minutes or until lightly browned. Remove from cookie sheets, and cool on wire racks. Yield: about 5½ dozen.

PEANUT BUTTER REFRIGERATOR COOKIES

½ cup butter or margarine,
  softened
1 cup chunky peanut butter
¾ cup sugar
½ cup firmly packed
  brown sugar
1 egg, lightly beaten
1 teaspoon vanilla extract
1¼ cups all-purpose flour
1½ teaspoons baking powder
¼ teaspoon salt

Cream butter and peanut butter in a large mixing bowl. Gradually add sugar, beating well. Beat in egg and vanilla.

Combine flour, baking powder, and salt; add to creamed mixture, stirring well.

Divide dough in half; shape each half into a roll, 2 inches in diameter. Wrap in waxed paper, and chill 3 hours or until firm.

Cut into ¼-inch slices; place 2 inches apart on ungreased cookie sheets. Bake at 350° for 10 minutes or until lightly browned. Remove from cookie sheets, and cool on wire racks. Yield: about 5 dozen.

GERMAN PECAN COOKIES

3¾ cups finely chopped
  pecans
3 cups all-purpose flour
2¼ cups sugar
2 teaspoons baking powder
1 tablespoon ground
  cinnamon
1 teaspoon ground nutmeg
½ teaspoon ground cloves
⅛ pound citron (optional)
3 eggs, lightly beaten
¼ cup plus 3 tablespoons
  butter or margarine, melted
1 egg white, lightly beaten

Combine pecans and dry ingredients in a large mixing bowl, stirring well to blend. Add citron, if desired, 3 eggs, and butter; mix well.

Shape dough into two 12-inch-long rolls; wrap in waxed paper, and chill until firm.

Cut into ¼-inch slices. Place 1 inch apart on lightly greased cookie sheets; brush tops of cookies with egg white. Bake at 350° for 10 to 12 minutes. Remove from cookie sheets, and cool on wire racks. Yield: about 6 dozen.

SHAPED AND PRESSED

Cookies come in an astonishing array of shapes, even without any cookie cutters on the premises. In short order, we can form bits of dough into crescents, logs, balls, pretzels — whatever whim and dexterity can create. Balls of dough may be flattened with the bottom of a glass dipped in sugar or flour or with the tines of a fork. Or we can put a thumbprint in each cookie and fill it with jelly.

The Southern cookie jar is filled with rich ethnic derivatives; their names sometimes give a clue to another homeland. Tuiles, baked and laid over a rolling pin while hot, take on a form very much like the French roofing tiles for which they are named. Buttery Spritz Cookies, formed with a press, are such a sweet habit that we tend to forget crediting them to the German immigrants who came to the South.

Some of our dressiest cookies are baked either on a griddle or in a special wafer iron and rolled into pipe or cone shapes. The most delicate of the little "pipes" can be rendered even more seductive by dipping the ends in chocolate. Two traditional European wafer irons are available: the Scandinavian krumkake iron, for a round, shallow, patterned cookie (ideal for making cones to be filled with icing or whipped cream) and the French *gaufrette* iron, for making the familiar honeycomb wafer. The early commercial version of the ice cream cone evolved from the krumkake iron. We may even bake a kind of cookie in the family waffle iron, not too unlike the one Thomas Jefferson brought back from France. Admittedly, his did not plug into an electrical outlet.

The old-fashioned rosette iron, with its several patterns, still gives us deep-fried pastries of cotton-candy lightness. There is even a spin-off of the traditional Mexican buñuelo, usually rolled thin and fried. With the dough thinned to a batter for dipping the rosette iron, the result is an even more gossamer buñuelo.

Flour, sugar, butter, eggs, and flavorings — we have had the makings of these shaped, shapely cookies all along. We just stopped calling them cakes and added a precious few flag-waving American ingredients such as pecans. Peanuts? They originated in South America, although excavations have placed them in Mexico two thousand years ago.

Southern cookies in various shapes. Clockwise from front plate: Snickerdoodles in cinnamon jackets, Bird's Nest Cookies with "eggs" of jelly, Porcupines with quills of coconut, French Cookies, and Pretzel Cookies, too!

FASHIONED BY WHIM

An entry for the Trade's Day Parade, San Antonio, 1910.

GREEK CINNAMON COOKIES

2 cups butter or margarine, softened
2 cups sugar
6 eggs
8¾ cups all-purpose flour, divided
1 tablespoon plus 2 teaspoons baking powder
1 teaspoon baking soda
1 teaspoon ground cinnamon
¼ cup olive oil
1 egg yolk, beaten

Cream butter in a large mixing bowl. Gradually add sugar, beating until light and fluffy. Add 6 eggs, one at a time, beating well after each addition.

Combine 3½ cups flour, baking powder, soda, and cinnamon in a medium mixing bowl; add to creamed mixture, stirring well. Add olive oil, mixing well. Add remaining flour, and stir until well blended.

Shape dough into 1½-inch balls, and place on lightly greased cookie sheets. Lightly brush tops of cookies with beaten egg yolk. Bake at 350° for 20 minutes. Cool slightly on cookie sheets; remove to a wire rack, and cool completely. Yield: about 7 dozen.

CHOCOLATE CRISPS

¼ cup shortening
3 (1-ounce) squares semisweet chocolate
1½ cups sugar
3 eggs
1¾ cups all-purpose flour
1½ teaspoons baking powder
1½ teaspoons vanilla extract
Powdered sugar

Combine shortening and chocolate in top of a double boiler; bring water to a boil. Reduce heat to low; cook until chocolate melts, stirring occasionally. Remove from heat; add 1½ cups sugar and eggs. Beat well with an electric mixer.

Sift together flour and baking powder in a small mixing bowl. Add half of flour mixture to chocolate mixture, stirring until well blended. Stir in vanilla. Add remaining flour mixture, stirring well.

Coat hands well with powdered sugar, and roll dough into 1-inch balls. Place 2 inches apart on lightly greased cookie sheets. Lightly sift powdered sugar over cookies.

Bake at 325° for 15 minutes. Cool slightly on cookie sheets. Remove to wire racks to cool completely. Yield: about 5 dozen.

SNICKERDOODLES

1 cup shortening
1½ cups plus 1 tablespoon sugar, divided
2 eggs
2¾ cups all-purpose flour
2 teaspoons cream of tartar
1 teaspoon baking soda
½ teaspoon salt
1 teaspoon vanilla extract
1 tablespoon ground cinnamon

Combine shortening, 1½ cups sugar, and eggs in a large mixing bowl, beating well.

Sift together flour, cream of tartar, soda, and salt in a small mixing bowl. Add flour mixture and vanilla to sugar mixture, stirring well.

Combine remaining sugar and cinnamon in a small mixing bowl, stirring well; set aside.

Shape dough into 1-inch balls; roll in reserved sugar-cinnamon mixture. Place on lightly greased cookie sheets; bake at 400° for 6 minutes or until lightly browned. Remove from cookie sheets, and cool on wire racks. Yield: about 4 dozen.

SEA ISLAND SPICE COOKIES

¾ cup butter or margarine
1 cup sugar
1 egg
¼ cup molasses
2 cups all-purpose flour
2 teaspoons baking soda
¼ teaspoon salt
1 teaspoon ground cinnamon
¾ teaspoon ground allspice
¾ teaspoon ground ginger
Sifted powdered sugar

Cream butter in a large mixing bowl; gradually add 1 cup sugar, beating until light and fluffy. Add egg and molasses; beat well.

Sift together flour, soda, salt, and spices; add to creamed mixture, stirring well.

Shape into 1-inch balls; place 2 inches apart on greased cookie sheets. Bake at 350° for 10 minutes or until lightly browned. Remove from cookie sheets, and cool completely on wire racks. Sprinkle with powdered sugar. Yield: 5½ dozen.

WALK-TO-SCHOOL COOKIES

3 cups butter or margarine, softened
2 cups sugar
1 cup crunchy nut-like cereal nuggets
2 teaspoons vanilla extract
6 cups all-purpose flour
Additional sugar

Cream butter in a large mixing bowl; gradually add 2 cups sugar, beating until light and fluffy. Add cereal and vanilla, mixing well; add flour, mixing until well blended.

Shape into 1½-inch balls; drop onto waxed paper that has been sprinkled with additional sugar.

Place balls, sugar-coated side down, 2 inches apart on ungreased cookie sheets. Gently press cookies with a fork in a crisscross pattern. Bake at 350° for 15 minutes. Remove from cookie sheets, and cool on wire racks. Yield: about 7 dozen.

Sea Island is but one of a chain of low, fertile islands off the coasts of South Carolina, Florida, and Georgia. The islands were claimed by Spain in 1516, but they eventually came under the rule of the British Crown. In 1717, they were granted to Sir Robert Montgomery, who called them The Golden Isles. The islands were looked upon as little kingdoms, privately held by individuals. Sea Island is still privately owned and is known worldwide as the site of the stunning Cloister Hotel. Some of the island's most imposing homes may be seen from Sea Island Drive.

"Walk-to-School" for a week on one batch of these cookies.

ALWAYS THE BEST.

DOES THEE EAT FRIENDS OATS

Trade card, 1890, for Muscatine's oats.

GUESS-AGAIN COOKIES

1 cup shortening
1 cup sugar
1 cup firmly packed
   brown sugar
2 eggs
2 cups all-purpose flour
½ teaspoon baking powder
1 teaspoon baking soda
½ teaspoon salt
2 cups oven-toasted rice
   cereal
2 cups regular oats, uncooked
1 cup raisins

Cream shortening in a large mixing bowl; gradually add sugar, beating well. Add eggs, beating well.

Combine flour, baking powder, soda, and salt in a medium mixing bowl; add to creamed mixture, stirring well. Stir in remaining ingredients; mix well.

Shape into 1-inch balls; place 2 inches apart on greased cookie sheets. Bake at 350° for 10 to 12 minutes. Remove from cookie sheets, and cool on wire racks. Yield: 8 dozen.

LEMON PRALINE COOKIES

¾ cup butter or margarine,
   softened
2 cups firmly packed
   brown sugar
2 eggs
2 teaspoons grated lemon
   rind
1 tablespoon lemon juice
2 cups all-purpose flour
1 cup finely chopped pecans

Cream butter in a medium mixing bowl; gradually add sugar, beating well. Add eggs, lemon rind, and juice; beat until well blended. Add flour and pecans to creamed mixture, stirring well. Cover and refrigerate overnight.

Shape into 1-inch balls; place 3 inches apart on greased cookie sheets. Bake at 375° for 6 to 8 minutes. Cool slightly on cookie sheets. Remove to wire racks, and cool completely. Yield: about 3 dozen.

OATMEAL CRINKLES

2 cups all-purpose flour
1 teaspoon baking powder
1 teaspoon baking soda
1 teaspoon salt
2½ cups regular oats,
   uncooked
1½ cups raisins
1¼ cups sugar, divided
1 teaspoon ground cinnamon
1 cup shortening
1 cup firmly packed
   brown sugar
2 eggs
1 teaspoon vanilla extract
¼ teaspoon almond extract

Combine flour, baking powder, soda, and salt in a medium mixing bowl; stir well, and set aside. Combine oats and raisins in a medium mixing bowl; set aside.

Combine ¼ cup sugar and cinnamon in a small mixing bowl; stir until well blended, and set aside.

Cream shortening in a large mixing bowl; add remaining 1 cup sugar, brown sugar, eggs, vanilla, and almond extract, beating until well blended.

Gradually add reserved flour and oats mixtures alternately to creamed mixture, stirring well after each addition.

Shape dough into 1-inch balls; roll in reserved sugar-cinnamon mixture, and place 2 inches apart on greased cookie sheets. Bake at 350° for 10 minutes. Cool slightly on cookie sheets. Remove to wire racks to cool completely. Yield: about 5 dozen.

BUTTER FINGERS

1 cup butter
¼ cup sugar
Dash of salt
1 teaspoon vanilla extract
1 cup finely chopped pecans
3 cups sifted all-purpose flour
Sifted powdered sugar

Cut butter into ¼ cup sugar and salt with a pastry blender; add vanilla and pecans, stirring well. Stir in flour. Mix well. (Dough will be crumbly.)

Shape into oblong fingers 2½- x ½-inch. Bake at 350° for 15 minutes; remove from oven, and immediately roll each cookie in powdered sugar. Cool completely on wire racks. Yield: about 2 dozen.

Pressing water from butter and packaging by the pound, c.1880.

PECAN SANDIES

2 cups butter, softened
¼ cup sifted powdered sugar
2 tablespoons water
1 tablespoon plus 1 teaspoon vanilla extract
4 cups all-purpose flour
2 cups chopped pecans
Additional powdered sugar

Cream butter; gradually add ¼ cup sugar, beating until light and fluffy. Add water and vanilla; beat well. Gradually stir in flour. Fold in pecans. Chill at least 1 hour.

Break off dough by heaping teaspoons, and shape into 2-inch crescents. Place on ungreased cookie sheets. Bake at 300° for 20 minutes. Remove immediately from cookie sheets, and coat with additional powdered sugar. Cool on wire racks. Yield: about 6 dozen.

PECAN DELIGHTS

1 cup butter, softened
¾ cup sugar, divided
1 tablespoon water
1 teaspoon vanilla extract
1¾ cups all-purpose flour
2 cups chopped pecans

Cream butter in a medium mixing bowl; add ½ cup sugar, water, and vanilla, beating well.

Combine flour and pecans in a small mixing bowl; stir well. Gradually add to creamed mixture, stirring well.

Pinch off small portions of dough, and shape like dates. Place 1 inch apart on ungreased cookie sheets, and bake at 325° for 25 minutes or until lightly browned. Remove from cookie sheets while still warm, and roll each cookie in remaining sugar. Place on wire racks to cool completely. Yield: about 4 dozen.

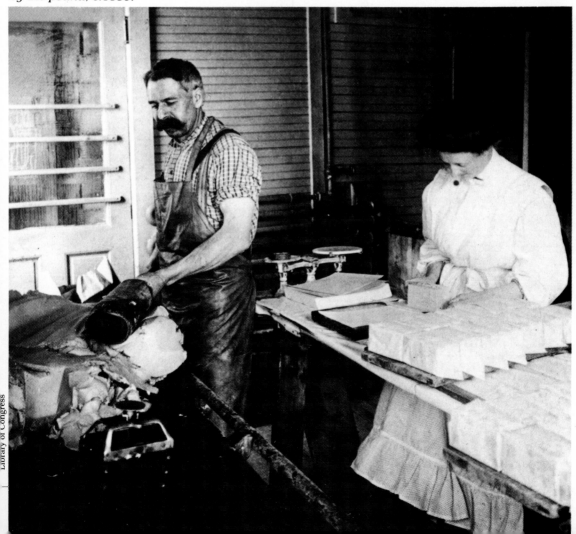

COCOA-NUT COOKIES

½ cup butter or margarine,
  softened
¼ cup sugar
1 teaspoon vanilla extract
1 cup sifted all-purpose flour
2 tablespoons Dutch Process
  cocoa
¾ cup finely chopped pecans
Sifted powdered sugar

Cream butter in a medium mixing bowl; gradually add sugar, beating until light and fluffy. Add vanilla, beating well. Add flour and cocoa to creamed mixture, stirring until well blended. Fold in pecans.

Shape into ½-inch balls; place on lightly greased cookie sheets. Bake at 350° for 12 to 15 minutes; cool slightly on cookie sheets. Remove to wire racks to cool completely. Roll in powdered sugar. Yield: about 3½ dozen.

*Kentucky Bourbon Cookies
are foolproof to make
and irresistible to eat.*

COCONUT BALLS

1 cup butter or margarine,
  softened
¼ cup sifted powdered sugar
1 tablespoon water
2 teaspoons vanilla extract
2 cups all-purpose flour
1 cup chopped pecans
4 cups sifted powdered sugar
½ cup milk
½ teaspoon vanilla extract
Dash of salt
1 (7-ounce) can flaked
  coconut

Cream butter in a large mixing bowl; gradually add ¼ cup sugar, beating until light and fluffy. Add water and 2 teaspoons vanilla, mixing well; add flour, stirring well. Stir in pecans.

Shape into ½-inch balls. Place 2 inches apart on ungreased cookie sheets; bake at 300° for 20 minutes or until lightly browned. Cool completely on cookie sheets.

Combine 4 cups sugar, milk, ½ teaspoon vanilla, and salt in a

medium mixing bowl; beat with a wire whisk until smooth.

Dip cookies in glaze; roll in coconut. Yield: 5 dozen.

Note: Coconut may be tinted, if desired.

KENTUCKY BOURBON COOKIES

1 (12-ounce) package vanilla
  wafers, finely crushed
1 cup sifted powdered sugar
2 tablespoons cocoa
1 cup chopped pecans
3 tablespoons light corn
  syrup
½ cup bourbon
Additional sifted powdered
  sugar

Combine wafer crumbs, 1 cup sugar, cocoa, and pecans in a large mixing bowl; stir well.

Combine syrup and bourbon, stirring well. Pour bourbon mixture over wafer mixture; mix well. Shape into 1-inch balls; roll in additional powdered sugar. Yield: 4½ dozen.

Helping Mother make cookies in one of those charming, nostalgic 1920s illustrations.

CRUNCHY SKILLET COOKIES

1 (8-ounce) package chopped dates
¾ cup sugar
½ cup butter or margarine
2 egg yolks, beaten
2 tablespoons milk
2 cups oven-toasted rice cereal
1 cup chopped pecans
2 teaspoons vanilla extract
1 cup flaked coconut

Combine dates, sugar, butter, egg yolks, and milk in a large skillet; cook over low heat 10 minutes, stirring constantly. Remove from heat; add cereal, pecans, and vanilla, mixing well. Cool slightly.

Shape into 1-inch balls; roll in coconut. Yield: 4 dozen.

PORCUPINES

2 cups chopped pecans
1 cup pitted dates
1½ cups grated coconut
1 cup firmly packed
   brown sugar
2 eggs
Additional grated coconut

Combine pecans and dates in the container of an electric blender; process until finely ground.

Combine pecan-date mixture, 1½ cups coconut, sugar, and eggs in a medium mixing bowl; mix well.

Drop by heaping teaspoonfuls into coconut, and roll into 3- x ½-inch oblong fingers. Place on lightly greased cookie sheets; bake at 350° for 10 to 12 minutes or until lightly browned. Remove from cookie sheets, and cool on wire racks. Yield: about 5 dozen.

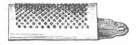

BIRD'S NEST COOKIES

1 cup butter or margarine,
   softened
½ cup sugar
½ cup firmly packed
   brown sugar
2 eggs, separated
½ teaspoon grated lemon rind
1 teaspoon lemon juice
½ teaspoon grated orange
   rind
½ teaspoon vanilla extract
¼ teaspoon salt
2 cups all-purpose flour
1¼ cups finely chopped
   pecans
Grape jelly

Cream butter in a large mixing bowl; gradually add sugar, beating until light and fluffy. Add egg yolks, beating well. Add lemon rind, juice, orange rind, vanilla, and salt; mix well. Sift flour; add to creamed mixture, mixing well.

Shape into 1-inch balls. Dip each ball in egg whites, and roll in pecans. Place 2 inches apart on ungreased cookie sheets; bake at 350° for 5 minutes.

Remove cookie sheets from oven, and quickly make an indention in the center of each cookie with the end of a wooden spoon handle. Return to oven, and bake an additional 8 minutes. Cool slightly on cookie sheets; remove cookies to wire racks, and cool completely. Fill the center of each cookie with jelly. Yield: about 3½ dozen.

EARLY AMERICAN PEANUT COOKIES

1 cup butter or margarine,
  softened
1 cup sugar
1 cup firmly packed
  brown sugar
2 eggs
2 teaspoons vanilla extract
1½ cups all-purpose flour
1 teaspoon baking soda
3 cups regular oats,
  uncooked
1½ cups salted peanuts

Cream butter in a large mixing bowl; gradually add sugar, beating well. Add eggs and vanilla; beat well. Combine flour and soda in a small mixing bowl; add to creamed mixture, mixing well. Stir in oats and peanuts.

Shape into 2½-inch balls; place 3 inches apart on greased cookie sheets. Flatten cookies with a fork in a crisscross pattern. Bake at 375° for 10 to 12 minutes. Cool slightly on cookie sheets; remove cookies to wire racks, and cool completely. Yield: about 1½ dozen.

PEANUT BLOSSOMS

½ cup shortening
½ cup sugar
½ cup firmly packed
  brown sugar
1 egg
2 tablespoons milk
1 teaspoon vanilla extract
½ cup creamy peanut butter
1¾ cups all-purpose flour
1 teaspoon baking soda
½ teaspoon salt
Milk chocolate candy kisses
Additional sugar

Cream shortening in a large mixing bowl; gradually add sugar, beating well. Add egg, milk, and vanilla; beat well. Stir in peanut butter.

Combine flour, soda, and salt in a medium mixing bowl; add to peanut butter mixture, stirring well. Shape into 1-inch balls. Roll in additional sugar, and place 2 inches apart on ungreased cookie sheets.

Bake at 375° for 10 minutes. Remove from oven; firmly press a candy kiss in center of each cookie. Remove to wire racks to cool. Yield: 4½ dozen.

The Europeans, arriving in Georgia, Tennessee, and North Carolina, were amazed at the Cherokees' ability to cultivate the land. The peanut, a staple in the Indian diet, was as obscure as the sweet potato in Europe. Peanuts arrived in North America via Peru. This valuable legume, call it goober, ground-nut, earth-nut, ground-pea, or pindar, grows in bush or vine form. It became a staple crop in the South after George Washington Carver pushed it as a money crop to replace cotton, wiped out by the boll weevil in the 1890s. Imagine life before peanut butter!

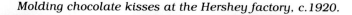
Molding chocolate kisses at the Hershey factory, c.1920.

PRETZEL COOKIES

1 cup butter, softened
2 cups sugar
4 eggs
4 cups all-purpose flour
1½ teaspoons baking
  powder
½ teaspoon ground
  cinnamon
½ teaspoon ground nutmeg
½ teaspoon ground cloves
1 cup ground pecans

Cream butter in a large mixing bowl; gradually add sugar, beating well. Add eggs, one at a time, beating well.

Combine flour, baking powder, and spices in a medium mixing bowl; add to creamed mixture, stirring well. Stir in pecans.

Shape dough into 1-inch balls. With floured hands, roll each ball into a rope, 10 to 12 inches long; twist ropes into pretzel shapes. Place 2 inches apart on greased cookie sheets.

Bake at 350° for 10 to 12 minutes. Remove pretzels from cookie sheets, and cool on wire racks. Yield: about 5 dozen.

rly American Peanut Cookies (left) and Peanut Blossoms.

MOTHER KEARNEY'S SUGAR-RAISIN COOKIES

1 cup lard, softened
2 cups sugar
2 eggs
4½ cups all-purpose flour
1 tablespoon plus 1 teaspoon
  baking powder
¼ teaspoon salt
1 teaspoon ground cinnamon
1 cup milk
Raisin Filling

Cream lard in a large mixing bowl; gradually add sugar, beating well. Add eggs, beating well.

Sift together dry ingredients in a medium mixing bowl. Add to creamed mixture alternately with milk, beginning and ending with flour mixture. Mix well after each addition.

Shape into 1½-inch balls; flatten each ball to ¼-inch thickness with lightly floured hands. Place raisin filling by heaping teaspoonfuls in centers of half the cookies. Moisten edges with water, and top with remaining cookies. Press edges together with a fork to seal.

Place on ungreased cookie sheets, and bake at 375° for 15 minutes or until lightly browned. Remove from cookie sheets, and cool on wire racks. Yield: about 2 dozen.

Raisin Filling:

¾ cup raisins
1¼ cups water, divided
¼ cup plus 2 tablespoons
  sugar
¼ teaspoon vanilla extract
1 tablespoon all-purpose flour

Combine raisins, 1 cup water, sugar, and vanilla in a medium saucepan, stirring well. Combine flour and remaining water, mixing well; add to raisin mixture, stirring well. Bring to a boil. Reduce heat; simmer, uncovered, stirring occasionally, 25 minutes or until thickened. Yield: about ¾ cup.

DATE SURPRISES

1 (8-ounce) package chopped
  dates
½ cup sugar
1 tablespoon lemon juice
½ cup water
1 cup shortening
1 cup firmly packed
  brown sugar
1 teaspoon baking soda
½ cup buttermilk
2 cups all-purpose flour
2 cups regular oats, uncooked
1 teaspoon salt

Combine first 4 ingredients in a saucepan; bring to a boil. Reduce heat, and cook over low heat 30 minutes or until thickened. Set aside to cool.

Cream shortening in a large mixing bowl; gradually add sugar, beating until light and fluffy. Dissolve soda in buttermilk, and add to creamed mixture, stirring well. Combine flour, oats, and salt; gradually add to creamed mixture, stirring well. Chill 2 hours.

Roll into 1-inch balls; place half of balls 2 inches apart on lightly greased cookie sheets. Press each ball into a 2½-inch circle. Spoon 1 teaspoon reserved date mixture onto circle. Shape remaining balls into 2½-inch circles, and place on top of date mixture; pinch edges together to seal. Bake at 325° for 12 to 15 minutes. Cool slightly, and remove to wire racks. Yield: about 2½ dozen.

Mrs. Benjamin Chew Howard's life was a busy one; she had twelve children and served as mistress of the Baltimore estate Belvidere. Famed for "elegant hospitality," she also directed the Great Southern Relief Association, benefiting Civil War victims. In 1873, she collected her recipes in *Fifty Years in a Maryland Kitchen*, again, for the benefit of charity.

STARLIGHT MINT SURPRISE COOKIES

1 cup butter, softened
1 cup sugar
½ cup firmly packed
  brown sugar
2 eggs
2 tablespoons water
1 teaspoon vanilla
  extract
3 cups all-purpose flour
1 teaspoon baking soda
½ teaspoon salt
Chocolate mint wafers
Pecan halves

Cream butter in a large mixing bowl; gradually add sugar, beating until light and fluffy. Add eggs, water, and vanilla, beating well.

Sift together flour, soda, and salt in a medium mixing bowl; add to creamed mixture, stirring well. Cover and refrigerate 2 hours or until thoroughly chilled.

Press 1 tablespoon dough to ¼-inch thickness with lightly floured hands; wrap around a mint, and place seam side down on a lightly greased cookie sheet. Gently press a pecan half on top of cookie. Repeat procedure with remaining dough, mints, and pecans. Bake at 375° for 10 minutes or until lightly browned. Remove from cookie sheets, and cool on wire racks. Yield: about 4 dozen.

Oil portrait of Mrs. Benjamin Chew Howard, 1801 to 1891.

Tuiles with Almonds really are shaped like roofing tiles!

MRS. B. C. HOWARD'S CINNAMON WAFERS

½ cup plus 2 tablespoons
  butter, softened
1⅓ cups powdered sugar,
  sifted
1 egg
1⅓ cups all-purpose flour
1 teaspoon ground cinnamon
1 cup milk

Cream butter in a medium mixing bowl; gradually add sugar, beating well. Add egg, beating well.

Sift together flour and cinnamon in a small mixing bowl; add to creamed mixture, stirring well. Gradually stir in milk.

For each wafer, pour 1 tablespoon batter onto a hot, lightly greased griddle, spreading thin with the back of a spoon. Cook until tops appear dry and edges begin to brown slightly. Turn and cook until bottom sides are browned. Remove from griddle, and wrap each wafer around the handle of a wooden spoon. Slide wafers off spoon handle, and cool seam side down on wire racks. Yield: about 4 dozen.

TUILES WITH ALMONDS

2 egg whites
½ cup sugar
½ cup blanched almonds,
  finely ground
½ cup all-purpose flour
¼ cup butter or margarine,
  melted
½ teaspoon almond extract
½ teaspoon vanilla extract

Combine egg whites (at room temperature) and ½ cup sugar in a medium mixing bowl; beat until mixture is foamy. Add ground almonds, flour, butter, and flavorings, stirring until well blended.

Drop by heaping teaspoonfuls 2 inches apart onto three well-greased cookie sheets. Use a fork dipped in water to flatten cookies.

Bake one sheet of cookies at a time at 350° for 8 minutes or just until lightly browned around the edges. Cool 30 seconds on cookie sheet; immediately loosen each cookie, and bend each around a rolling pin. Press gently against the pin for a few seconds. Slide molded

wafers off pin, and place on wire racks to cool completely. Repeat baking and shaping procedure with cookies on remaining cookie sheets. Store cookies in an airtight container. Yield: about 2½ dozen.

Promotional picture for an early waffle iron, c.1920.

FRENCH COOKIES

5 eggs, separated
6¾ cups all-purpose flour
2 cups sugar
2 cups firmly packed
    brown sugar
⅛ teaspoon baking powder
2 cups butter, melted
1 teaspoon vanilla extract

Beat egg yolks in a small mixing bowl until thick and lemon colored. Set aside. Beat egg whites (at room temperature) in a medium mixing bowl until foamy; set aside.

Combine flour, sugar, and baking powder in a large mixing bowl; mix until well blended. Stir in butter, reserved egg yolks, and vanilla. Fold in egg whites, blending well. Cover and refrigerate overnight.

Shape dough into 1-inch balls. Bake, a few at a time, in a preheated, lightly oiled waffle iron until golden brown. Cool on wire racks, and store in airtight containers. Yield: about 11 dozen.

Note: Dough may be shaped into balls, frozen, and thawed to bake when desired.

BUÑUELO ROSETTES

½ cup plus 2 teaspoons
    sugar, divided
1 teaspoon ground cinnamon
2 eggs, lightly beaten
1 cup milk
¼ teaspoon salt
1 cup all-purpose flour
1 teaspoon lemon extract
Vegetable oil

Combine ½ cup sugar and cinnamon in a small mixing bowl; mix well, and set aside.

Combine eggs, milk, remaining sugar, and salt in a medium mixing bowl; mix well. Add flour, and beat with a wire whisk until smooth. Stir in lemon extract, mixing well.

Dip rosette iron into hot oil (375°); drain off excess oil. Dip hot iron halfway into batter; return to oil, and cook 30 seconds. Buñuelo will slip off rosette iron after 10 to 15 seconds. Turn buñuelo occasionally. Remove with slotted spoon; drain on paper towels. Sprinkle with reserved sugar-cinnamon mixture. Repeat procedure with remaining batter. Yield: about 4 dozen.

ROLLED SWEET WAFERS

½ cup butter or margarine,
    softened
⅔ cup sugar
1 egg
1 cup all-purpose flour
½ cup milk
1 teaspoon vanilla extract
Vegetable oil

Cream butter in a medium mixing bowl; gradually add sugar, beating until light and fluffy. Add egg; beat well. Add flour alternately with milk, beginning and ending with flour. Mix well after each addition. Stir in vanilla.

Brush pizelle or waffle iron with oil; preheat iron 2 minutes. Place 1 heaping teaspoon of batter in center of iron; close iron, and bake 1 minute or until lightly browned. Remove wafer, and quickly roll up; cool on a wire rack. Repeat procedure with remaining batter. Store wafers in an airtight container. Yield: about 2½ dozen.

Note: These wafers are delicious served with ice cream.

PRESS TO SHAPE

BASIC PRESSED COOKIES

1 cup butter, softened
⅔ cup sugar
1 egg
1 teaspoon almond extract
2½ cups all-purpose flour
½ teaspoon baking powder
⅛ teaspoon salt

Cream butter in a medium mixing bowl; gradually add sugar, beating until light and fluffy. Add egg and almond extract; beat well.

Combine flour, baking powder, and salt in a small mixing bowl; gradually add to creamed mixture, stirring well after each addition.

Press dough from a cookie press onto ungreased cookie sheets, following manufacturer's instructions. Bake at 400° for 6 to 8 minutes. Remove from cookie sheets, and cool on wire racks. Yield: about 4 dozen.

THE COOKY JAR
As soon as school is out at night,
All children, near and far,
Go rushing home, in one mad flight,
To find the Cooky Jar!
(So keep it filled for their delight;
You know how children are.)

SPRITZ COOKIES

1 cup shortening
¾ cup sugar
1 egg
1 teaspoon vanilla extract
2¼ cups all-purpose flour
½ teaspoon baking powder
¼ teaspoon salt
Frosting (recipe follows)

Cream shortening in a medium mixing bowl; gradually add sugar, beating until light and fluffy. Add egg and vanilla, beating well.

Sift together flour, baking powder, and salt in a small mixing bowl; gradually add to creamed mixture, stirring well after each addition.

Press dough from a cookie press onto ungreased cookie sheets, using desired shaping disks. Bake at 350° for 12 to 15 minutes. Remove from cookie sheets, and cool completely on wire racks.

Spoon frosting into a pastry bag fitted with a star tip; decorate each cookie as desired. Yield: about 5½ dozen.

Frosting:

⅔ cup shortening
¼ teaspoon salt
½ teaspoon almond or vanilla extract
⅓ cup water
1 (16-ounce) package powdered sugar, sifted
Paste food coloring (optional)

Combine shortening, salt, and desired flavoring in a medium mixing bowl; beat at medium speed of an electric mixer until well blended. Add water alternately with powdered sugar, beating constantly at low speed until smooth. Beat an additional 8 minutes at medium speed.

Color portions of frosting with paste food coloring, if desired. Yield: frosting for 5½ dozen cookies.

Note: Frosting may be stored at room temperature or in refrigerator for several days.

DOUBLE-DIP NUT FINGERS

1¼ cups butter or margarine, softened
¾ cup sugar
1 egg
2 teaspoons grated orange rind
3¼ cups all-purpose flour
½ teaspoon baking powder
¼ teaspoon salt
1 (6-ounce) package semisweet chocolate morsels
¼ cup plus 2 tablespoons whipping cream
Chopped pecans
Shredded coconut
Colored sugar

Cream butter in a large mixing bowl; gradually add sugar, beating until light and fluffy. Add egg and orange rind; beat well. Sift together flour, baking powder, and salt in a medium mixing bowl; add to creamed mixture, mixing well.

Press dough from a cookie press onto ungreased cookie sheets, making 3-inch long cookies. Bake at 400° for 5 to 7 minutes. Remove cookies to wire racks, and cool completely.

Place chocolate in top of a double boiler; bring water to a boil. Reduce heat to low; cook just until chocolate melts. Remove from heat, and cool slightly. Gradually add whipping cream to melted chocolate, stirring until well blended.

Dip ends of cookies in chocolate, covering ½ inch on each end. Sprinkle ends with pecans, coconut, or colored sugar. Cool cookies on wire racks until chocolate is firm. Yield: about 7 dozen.

OLD-FASHIONED SUGAR 'N SPICE COOKIES

½ cup butter, softened
¾ cup sugar
¾ cup firmly packed
  brown sugar
2 eggs
Juice of 1 lemon
1 teaspoon vanilla extract
3 cups all-purpose flour
½ teaspoon baking soda
½ teaspoon ground cinnamon
¼ teaspoon ground allspice

Cream butter in a large mixing bowl; gradually add sugar, beating well. Add eggs, one at a time, beating well after each addition. Add lemon juice and vanilla; mix well.

Sift together flour, soda, cinnamon, and allspice in a medium mixing bowl; gradually add to creamed mixture, stirring well after each addition.

Press dough from a cookie press onto lightly greased cookie sheets, making 12-inch ribbon-like strips. Bake at 350° for 8 minutes or until edges are lightly browned.

Cut each 12-inch strip into 3-inch segments while warm. Carefully remove from cookie sheets, and cool on wire racks. Yield: about 9 dozen.

CARAMEL PRESS COOKIES

1 cup butter, softened
¾ cup firmly packed
  brown sugar
1 egg yolk
½ teaspoon vanilla extract
¼ teaspoon salt
2 cups all-purpose flour

Cream butter in a large mixing bowl; gradually add sugar, beating until light and fluffy. Add egg yolk, vanilla, and salt; beat well. Stir in flour. Chill at least 1 hour.

Press dough from cookie press onto ungreased cookie sheets. Bake at 350° for 8 to 10 minutes. Remove cookies to wire racks to cool. Yield: about 5 dozen.

Double-Dip Nut Fingers (front) and Sugar 'n Spice Cookies.

OF BARS AND SQUARES

Brownie lovers, your patience is about to be rewarded, but in good time. To be chronological about it, brownies developed later than some of the other bar cookies. Besides, un-chocolate cookies, to be democratic about it, can be sensational too. Early recipe writers are so chary with their instructions that it is difficult to say when the bake-and-cut cookie arrived. On occasion, however, a clue turns up: When the instructions say, " . . . or add more flour, roll out and cut," we could infer that the dough would make a bar cookie if pressed into a pan. But Southern cooks in a hurry have always known how to short-cut a recipe without having it spelled out.

Tea cakes, in the cookbooks of the 1800s, are assumed to be rolled and cut for baking. *Housekeeping in the Blue-grass*, 1875, however, contains a cup cake we would recognize as a bar cookie: "Bake in a quick oven; when cold, ice it, and cut in squares." It was called "cup cake" just because of the cup used to measure the ingredients. Some cup cakes were baked in "hoops" to become layer cakes.

Brownies, according to John F. Mariani in *The Dictionary of American Food and Drink*, first appear in print in a Sears, Roebuck & Company catalogue in 1897. Their popularity gathered such momentum early in the twentieth century that bar cookies that were not brownies were called "blonde" or "butterscotch" brownies.

The evolution of chocolate from the Aztecs' bitter aphrodisiac to the varied, refined forms we use today is another, very long story. We can flavor our brownies with either cocoa, unsweetened baking chocolate, chocolate syrup, chocolate chips, or German's Sweet Chocolate . . . named for Sam German, who developed the confection while working for the Walter Baker Company in 1852.

Our brownies may turn out chewy or cake-light or even crisp — as we like them. And we don't always have to cut them into squares. Fingers or bars are nice, but some cooks lean to the diamond shape, as it allows the work force to munch up all the sides and corners that don't conform to the pattern. The chocolate lover's credo might be, "You can't be sure you've found your favorite brownie until you have tried them all." A pleasurable, never-ending quest.

Clockwise from front: London Bars, German Cream Cheese Brownies, Glazed Cinnamon Cookies. When we opt for the angle-cut cookie, we take a legitimate shortcut to a delicious result.

FRUIT AND NUT MEDLEY

Postcard showing a Florida banana plantation, 1920.

BANANA BARS

1 small ripe banana, mashed
¼ cup shortening
1 egg
1 cup all-purpose flour
¾ cup sugar
½ teaspoon baking powder
¼ teaspoon baking soda
½ teaspoon salt
¾ teaspoon ground cinnamon
¼ teaspoon ground allspice
⅛ teaspoon ground cloves
¼ cup milk
⅓ cup chopped pecans
Lemon Frosting

Combine banana and shortening in a medium mixing bowl; beat at high speed of an electric mixer 2 minutes. Add egg, and beat 1 minute.

Sift together flour, sugar, baking powder, soda, salt, and spices in a small mixing bowl; add to banana mixture, stirring well. Stir in milk and pecans.

Pour batter into a lightly greased 13- x 9- x 2-inch baking pan; bake at 350° for 20 to 25 minutes or until a wooden pick inserted in center comes out clean. Spread with Lemon Frosting while warm; cool completely. Cut into 2- x 1½-inch bars to serve. Yield: about 3 dozen.

Lemon Frosting:

1 cup sifted powdered sugar
2 tablespoons butter or margarine, melted
1 tablespoon water
2 teaspoons lemon juice

Combine sugar, butter, water, and lemon juice; beat with a wire whisk until smooth. Yield: frosting for 3 dozen bars.

APPLE SPICE BARS

½ cup shortening
1 cup sugar
3 eggs, beaten
1 cup all-purpose flour
1 teaspoon baking powder
½ teaspoon salt
1 teaspoon ground cinnamon
½ teaspoon ground nutmeg
¼ teaspoon ground cloves
1 cup regular oats, uncooked
1½ cups chopped, peeled apple
½ cup raisins
½ cup chopped pecans
Sifted powdered sugar

Cream shortening in a large mixing bowl; gradually add 1 cup sugar, beating well. Add eggs, and beat well. Sift together flour, baking powder, salt, and spices in a small mixing bowl; gradually add to creamed mixture, stirring well. Stir in next 4 ingredients, mixing well.

Press mixture into a greased 15- x 10- x 1-inch jellyroll pan. Bake at 350° for 25 minutes. Cool; sprinkle with powdered sugar, and cut into 2- x 1-inch bars. Yield: about 6 dozen.

BUTTER CRISPS

½ cup butter, softened
½ cup margarine, softened
1 cup sugar
1 egg, separated
2 teaspoons vanilla extract
2 cups all-purpose flour
Dash of salt
1 cup finely chopped pecans

Cream butter and margarine in a large mixing bowl; gradually add sugar, beating until light and fluffy. Add egg yolk; beat well. Stir in vanilla. Add flour and salt to creamed mixture; stir well.

Press dough into a greased 15- x 10- x 1-inch jellyroll pan; brush with egg white. Sprinkle pecans on top. Bake at 350° for 30 minutes or until lightly browned. Cut into 2- x 1-inch bars while warm. Yield: about 6 dozen.

BUTTERSCOTCH-FRUIT SQUARES

½ cup butter or margarine,
  softened
¾ cup firmly packed
  brown sugar
1 egg
½ teaspoon vanilla extract
1¼ cups all-purpose flour
½ teaspoon baking soda
½ teaspoon salt
Filling (recipe follows)
1 (6-ounce) package
  butterscotch morsels
¾ cup mixed candied fruit
½ cup chopped walnuts

Cream butter; gradually add sugar, beating well. Add egg and vanilla, beating until smooth. Combine flour, soda, and salt; stir into creamed mixture. Spread evenly in a lightly greased 13- x 9- x 2-inch baking pan. Bake at 350° for 15 minutes. Cool in pan 10 minutes.

Spread filling evenly over crust. Combine remaining ingredients; sprinkle over filling. Bake at 350° an additional 15 minutes. Cool and cut into 2-inch squares. Yield: about 2 dozen.

Filling:

2 tablespoons firmly packed
  brown sugar
2 tablespoons milk
1 tablespoon butter or
  margarine, melted
1 egg
⅓ cup all-purpose flour
½ teaspoon baking soda
¼ teaspoon salt
½ teaspoon ground cinnamon

Combine sugar, milk, butter, and egg in a small mixing bowl. Beat at medium speed of an electric mixer until smooth. Combine flour, soda, salt, and cinnamon; add to sugar mixture, beating until smooth. Yield: about ⅔ cup.

GLAZED CINNAMON COOKIES

1 cup butter or margarine,
  softened
1⅓ cups sugar, divided
1 egg, separated
¼ teaspoon vanilla extract
1¾ cups all-purpose flour
½ teaspoon salt
1 teaspoon ground cinnamon,
  divided
1 tablespoon cold water
½ cup finely chopped pecans

Cream butter in a large mixing bowl; gradually add 1 cup sugar, beating until light and fluffy. Add egg yolk and vanilla; beat well.

Combine flour, salt, and ½ teaspoon cinnamon in a small mixing bowl, stirring well. Gradually add to creamed mixture, stirring well after each addition. Press dough evenly into an ungreased 15- x 10- x 1-inch jellyroll pan; set aside.

Combine egg white (at room temperature), remaining sugar and cinnamon, and cold water in a small mixing bowl; beat lightly with a fork. Brush evenly over dough in pan; sprinkle with pecans. Bake at 300° for 45 minutes. Cool slightly in pan. Cut into 3- x 2-inch bars; remove to wire racks to cool completely. Store cookies in an airtight container. Yield: about 2 dozen.

Ad for Washburn-Crosby Company's Gold Medal Flour.

*Busy dock scene of
workers unloading a cargo
of coconuts from a Gulf
and Southern Steamship
Company schooner, 1919.*

HELLO DOLLY BARS

¼ cup butter or margarine
1 cup graham cracker crumbs
1 (7-ounce) can flaked
  coconut
1 (6-ounce) package
  semisweet chocolate
  morsels
1 (6-ounce) package
  butterscotch morsels
1 cup chopped pecans
1 (14-ounce) can sweetened
  condensed milk

Melt butter in a 13- x 9- x 2-
inch baking pan. Sprinkle
cracker crumbs evenly over butter. Layer next 4 ingredients
evenly over cracker crumbs in
order listed. Spoon sweetened
condensed milk over top of
layers. Bake at 350° for 30 minutes. Cool and cut into 3- x 1-
inch bars. Yield: about 3 dozen.

COCONUT PIE BARS

½ cup butter or margarine,
  softened
1¾ cups firmly packed brown
  sugar, divided
1½ cups all-purpose flour,
  divided
½ teaspoon baking powder
2 eggs, beaten
½ teaspoon vanilla extract
1 cup flaked coconut
1 cup chopped pecans

Combine butter and ¼ cup
brown sugar, creaming until
light and fluffy. Add 1 cup flour,
and mix well. Press mixture
evenly into a lightly greased 9-
inch square baking pan. Bake
at 350° for 15 minutes.

Combine remaining sugar,
flour, and baking powder in a
large mixing bowl; stir in eggs
and vanilla, mixing well. Add coconut and pecans; stir well.

Spread coconut mixture
evenly over baked mixture. Bake
at 350° for 25 minutes. Cool and
cut into 2- x 1-inch bars. Yield:
about 3 dozen.

COCONUT COOKIES

1½ cups all-purpose flour
½ cup sugar
¾ cup butter or margarine
3 eggs, separated
2 cups firmly packed
  brown sugar
1 cup flaked coconut
1 cup chopped pecans

Combine flour and ½ cup
sugar in a large mixing bowl;
cut in butter with a pastry
blender until mixture resembles
coarse meal. Press mixture
evenly into a greased 13- x 9- x
2-inch baking pan. Bake at 325°
for 20 minutes or until set.

Beat egg yolks in a medium
mixing bowl. Stir in remaining
ingredients, except egg whites.

Beat egg whites (at room temperature) until stiff peaks form.
Fold into coconut mixture.
Spread mixture evenly over
baked crust. Bake at 400° for 10
minutes; reduce heat to 350°,
and bake an additional 20 minutes. Cool and cut into 1½-inch
squares. Yield: 4 dozen.

COCONUT VANITIES

¼ cup butter or margarine,
  softened
1 tablespoon grated orange
  rind
1½ cups sugar, divided
1 egg
2 cups sifted cake flour
2 teaspoons baking powder
¼ teaspoon salt
½ cup orange juice
¼ cup milk
2 egg whites
2 cups flaked coconut

Cream butter in a large mixing bowl; add orange rind and 1 cup sugar, beating well. Add 1 egg; beat well.

Sift flour, baking powder, and salt 3 times in a medium mixing bowl; gradually add to creamed mixture alternately with juice and milk, beginning and ending with flour mixture; stir well after each addition. Spread mixture evenly in a greased 15- x 10- x 1-inch jellyroll pan.

Beat 2 egg whites (at room temperature) in a small mixing bowl until foamy; gradually add remaining sugar, beating until well blended. Very gently spread meringue mixture evenly over entire surface of batter; sprinkle with coconut. Bake at 350° for 20 minutes. Remove from oven, and cool completely in pan before cutting with a 2½- x 2-inch diamond-shaped cutter. Yield: about 2 dozen.

The coconut palm grows wherever the seeds are carried by the oceans that wash tropical shores, including Florida. Southerners have been eating coconut for ages. But why is the coconut the "most useful tree in the world?" Island cultures depend on it for thatch, baskets, oars, drink, rope: the basics. Its oil was used in ancient times; it still is, in margarine and soap.

COCONUT-ORANGE SQUARES

½ cup butter or margarine
1½ cups sugar
2 eggs
2 teaspoons grated orange
  rind
¼ cup orange juice
3 cups flaked coconut,
  divided
1½ cups all-purpose flour
1 teaspoon baking powder
¼ teaspoon salt

Cream butter in a large mixing bowl; gradually add sugar, beating well. Add eggs, orange rind, juice, and 2 cups coconut; stir well. Combine flour, baking powder, and salt; stir into creamed mixture.

Spread batter evenly in a greased and floured 13- x 9- x 2-inch baking pan. Sprinkle with remaining coconut. Bake at 350° for 25 to 30 minutes. Cool completely in pan; cut into 2-inch squares. Yield: about 2 dozen.

Coconut-Orange Squares laden with tropical flavors.

When Gottlieb's Bakery celebrated its centennial year in 1984, all Savannah glowed with pride. Isadore Gottlieb, a Russian immigrant, started the business by peddling baked goods on foot, then by wagon. Three moves later, the bakery expanded over an entire block on Bull Street, with outlets in Oglethorpe Mall and on Hilton Head Island.

Bay Street in Savannah, Georgia, looking east from City Hall, c. 1905. Gottlieb's Bakery Fruit Bars (below).

GOTTLIEB'S BAKERY FRUIT BARS

½ cup shortening
1¼ cups sugar
1 egg
1 teaspoon vanilla extract
2¼ cups all-purpose flour
1 teaspoon baking soda
½ teaspoon salt
1 teaspoon ground cinnamon
1 teaspoon ground allspice
⅓ cup water
1½ cups raisins
1 cup yellow cake crumbs
1 cup sifted powdered sugar
2 tablespoons water

Cream shortening in a large mixing bowl; gradualy add 1¼ cups sugar, beating well. Add egg; beat well. Stir in vanilla.

Combine flour, soda, salt, cinnamon, and allspice; gradually add to creamed mixture alternately with ⅓ cup water, beginning and ending with flour mixture. Stir in raisins and cake crumbs.

Divide dough into 4 equal portions. With floured hands, roll each portion into a 6-inch log. Place 3 inches apart on well-greased cookie sheets; slightly flatten each log. Bake at 350° for 20 minutes.

Combine powdered sugar and 2 tablespoons water in a small mixing bowl; beat until smooth. Drizzle glaze over tops of warm cookies. Slice into bars with a warm knife. Cool on cookie sheets 5 minutes. Remove to wire racks to cool completely. Yield: about 4½ dozen.

DREAM BARS

¾ cup butter, softened
¼ cup firmly packed light
  brown sugar
¼ cup firmly packed dark
  brown sugar
1½ cups all-purpose flour
1 (16-ounce) carton
  commercial sour cream
1 tablespoon plus 1½
  teaspoons sugar
1½ teaspoons vanilla extract
Red maraschino cherries,
  halved

Cream butter in a large mixing bowl; add brown sugar, and beat until light and fluffy. Gradually add flour, mixing well. Press mixture evenly into an ungreased 13- x 9- x 2-inch baking pan. Bake at 350° for 25 minutes; remove from oven, and set aside.

Combine sour cream, 1 tablespoon plus 1½ teaspoons sugar, and vanilla; beat at medium speed of an electric mixer until well blended. Spread evenly over baked mixture. Bake an additional 10 minutes. Cool completely in pan. Cut into 3- x 1½-inch bars; remove from pan, and garnish each bar with a cherry half. Yield: about 2 dozen.

DIXIE DATE BARS

¼ cup butter or margarine,
  melted
½ cup sugar
1 egg, lightly beaten
½ cup all-purpose flour
½ teaspoon baking powder
¼ teaspoon salt
1 cup chopped dates
¼ cup chopped pecans

Combine butter and sugar in a medium mixing bowl; stir well. Add egg; stir until smooth. Combine flour, baking powder, and salt; add to sugar mixture. Fold in dates and pecans.

Spoon batter into a greased and floured 9-inch square baking pan. Bake at 325° for 30 minutes. Cool slightly in pan; cut into 2- x 1-inch bars. Remove to wire racks to cool completely. Yield: about 3 dozen.

Well-trained young beekeeper shows off his expertise.

HARD HONEY COOKIES

1 cup sugar
½ cup honey
1 egg
1 teaspoon ground cinnamon
½ teaspoon ground cloves
¼ teaspoon ground ginger
Dash of salt
½ teaspoon baking soda
1 tablespoon water
2¼ cups all-purpose flour
½ cup slivered almonds

Combine sugar and honey in a large mixing bowl, beating well. Add egg, cinnamon, cloves, ginger, and salt; beat well.

Dissolve soda in water; add to honey mixture, stirring well. Stir in flour and almonds.

Press dough evenly into a greased and floured 13- x 9- x 2-inch baking pan. Bake at 350° for 20 to 25 minutes. Cut into 3- x 1-inch bars. Remove cookies to wire racks to cool completely. Yield about 3 dozen.

Note: Cookies may be stored 3 to 4 weeks in a cake tin with an apple to mellow.

LONDON BARS

¾ cup butter or margarine,
  softened
1¼ cups sugar, divided
4 eggs, separated
2¼ cups all-purpose flour
1 (12-ounce) jar raspberry
  preserves
1 teaspoon vanilla extract
½ cup chopped pecans

Cream butter in a large mixing bowl; gradually add ¼ cup sugar, beating until light and fluffy. Add egg yolks, one at a time, beating well after each addition. Stir in flour.

Press mixture into a lightly greased 15- x 10- x 1-inch jellyroll pan. Bake at 350° for 25 minutes or until lightly browned. Remove from oven; cool in pan. Spread preserves over baked crust.

Beat egg whites (at room temperature) in a medium mixing bowl until foamy. Gradually add remaining sugar, 1 tablespoon at a time, beating until stiff peaks form. Fold in vanilla. Spread meringue over preserves. Sprinkle with pecans.

Bake at 350° for 15 minutes or until lightly browned. Cool slightly; cut into 2- x 1-inch bars with a warm knife. Yield: about 6 dozen.

These gentlemen are checking the harvest in this eight-year-old orange grove, c.1910.

SWEDISH ORANGE-NUT SQUARES

½ cup butter or margarine, softened
¼ cup sugar
3 tablespoons grated orange rind, divided
1 egg
1¼ cups plus 2 tablespoons all-purpose flour, divided
1½ cups firmly packed brown sugar
2 eggs, beaten
2 tablespoons orange juice
½ teaspoon baking powder
⅔ cup flaked coconut
⅔ cup chopped pecans
Sifted powdered sugar

Cream butter in a medium mixing bowl; gradually add ¼ cup sugar, 1 tablespoon orange rind, and 1 egg. Stir in 1¼ cups flour. Spread mixture evenly in a greased 9-inch square baking pan. Bake at 350° for 20 minutes or until set.

Combine brown sugar and 2 eggs in a large mixing bowl, beating well. Add 2 tablespoons orange rind and juice; stir well. Stir in remaining 2 tablespoons flour and baking powder. Fold in coconut and pecans. Pour mixture evenly over baked crust. Bake at 350° for 20 to 25 minutes. Sprinkle with powdered sugar, and cut into 1½-inch squares. Cool completely in pan. Yield: 3 dozen.

LEMON SQUARES

2¼ cups all-purpose flour, divided
½ cup sifted powdered sugar
1 cup butter or margarine, melted
4 eggs, beaten
2 cups sugar
⅓ cup lemon juice
½ teaspoon baking powder
Additional sifted powdered sugar

Combine 2 cups flour and ½ cup powdered sugar; add butter, mixing well. Press mixture evenly into a 13- x 9- x 2-inch baking dish. Bake at 350° for 20 minutes.

Combine eggs, sugar, and lemon juice in a medium mixing bowl; beat well. Sift together ¼ cup flour and baking powder in a medium mixing bowl; stir into egg mixture. Pour over baked crust. Bake at 350° for 25 minutes or until lightly browned and set. Sprinkle lightly with additional powdered sugar. Cool and cut into 1-inch squares. Yield: about 10 dozen.

MUD HENS

½ cup butter or margarine, softened
1 cup sugar
1 egg
1 egg, separated
½ teaspoon vanilla extract
1½ cups all-purpose flour
1 teaspoon baking powder
½ teaspoon salt
1 cup chopped pecans
1 cup firmly packed brown sugar

Cream butter in a large mixing bowl; gradually add 1 cup sugar, beating well. Add 1 egg and egg yolk; beat well. Stir in vanilla.

Combine flour, baking powder, and salt in a small mixing bowl; add to creamed mixture, stirring well. Press into a greased 13- x 9- x 2-inch baking pan; sprinkle with chopped pecans.

Beat egg white (at room temperature) in a small mixing bowl until foamy. Gradually add brown sugar, 1 tablespoon at a time, beating until stiff peaks form and sugar dissolves. (Do not underbeat mixture.) Spread evenly over pecans.

Bake at 350° for 30 minutes or until lightly browned. Cool completely in pan. Cut into 2-inch squares. Yield: about 2 dozen.

ORANGE SLICE BARS

½ cup butter or margarine, melted
2 cups firmly packed brown sugar
4 eggs, beaten
2 cups all-purpose flour
1 pound candy orange slices, finely chopped
1 cup chopped pecans
1 cup sifted powdered sugar

Combine butter and brown sugar in a large mixing bowl; stir in eggs, mixing well. Add flour, chopped orange slices, and pecans; stir until well blended.

Pour batter into a well-greased 15- x 10- x 1-inch jellyroll pan. Bake at 350° for 25 minutes. Cool 15 minutes in pan; cut into 2- x 2-inch squares. Cool completely in pan. Remove bars from pan; cut in half diagonally, and roll in powdered sugar. Yield: 6 dozen.

CRUNCHY PEANUT BAR COOKIES

1 cup whipping cream
1 cup sugar
1 cup light corn syrup
1 tablespoon butter or margarine
6 cups corn flakes cereal
2 cups oven-toasted rice cereal
2 cups salted peanuts

Combine whipping cream, sugar, syrup, and butter in a 3-quart saucepan; cook over low heat, stirring constantly, until sugar dissolves. Cook over medium heat, without stirring, until mixture registers 232° (thread stage) on a candy thermometer. Remove from heat.

Combine cereal and peanuts in a large mixing bowl. Pour hot sugar mixture over cereal mixture, stirring well to combine. Press firmly into a greased 13- x 9- x 2-inch baking pan, using back of spoon. Cool and cut into 2- x 1-inch bars. Yield: about 5 dozen.

PEANUT BUTTER CRUNCHIES

1 cup sugar
1 cup corn syrup
1 cup smooth peanut butter
6 cups oven-toasted rice cereal
1 (6-ounce) package semisweet chocolate morsels
1 (6-ounce) package butterscotch morsels

Combine sugar and syrup in a small saucepan; bring to a boil. Remove from heat; add peanut butter, stirring until smooth.

Combine peanut butter mixture and cereal; mix well. Press mixture evenly into a lightly greased 13- x 9- x 2-inch baking pan, using back of spoon.

Combine chocolate and butterscotch morsels in top of a double boiler; cook over simmering water, stirring constantly, until morsels melt. Spread evenly over mixture in pan. Chill; cut into 1½-inch squares. Yield: about 4 dozen.

Orange Slice Bars, the candy lover's cookies.

A scrupulously clean peanut butter packing plant, c.1910.

NO-BAKE PEANUT BUTTER BARS

1¼ cups graham cracker
   crumbs
¼ cup sugar
½ teaspoon ground cinnamon
¾ cup plus 2 tablespoons
   chunky peanut butter,
   divided
⅓ cup corn syrup
1 (6-ounce) package
   semisweet chocolate
   morsels

Combine cracker crumbs, sugar, and cinnamon in a medium mixing bowl; add ¾ cup peanut butter and syrup, mixing just until blended. Press mixture evenly into an 8-inch square baking pan; set aside.

Place chocolate morsels in top of a double boiler; place over simmering water, and stir until chocolate melts. Spread chocolate evenly over surface of peanut butter mixture. Swirl remaining peanut butter in warm chocolate; set aside until chocolate cools completely. Cut into 4- x 1-inch bars. Yield: about 1½ dozen.

KATHLEEN DANIELSON'S PECAN STRIPS

½ cup butter, softened
1 cup plus 1 tablespoon
   all-purpose flour, divided
¾ cup firmly packed
   brown sugar
1 egg
¼ teaspoon baking powder
¼ teaspoon salt
½ teaspoon vanilla extract
¼ cup flaked coconut
½ cup coarsely chopped
   pecans
1½ cups sifted powdered
   sugar
Dash of salt
1 to 2 tablespoons lemon
   juice

Cream butter in a medium mixing bowl. Gradually add 1 cup flour; beat at medium speed of an electric mixer until mixture resembles coarse crumbs. Continue beating until mixture forms a smooth paste. Press evenly in a lightly greased 9-inch square baking pan. Bake at 350° for 12 minutes. Remove from oven; set aside.

Combine brown sugar, egg, remaining flour, baking powder, ¼ teaspoon salt, vanilla, coconut, and pecans in a medium mixing bowl; mix until well blended. Spread evenly over baked mixture in pan. Return to oven, and bake an additional 20 minutes. Set aside to cool completely in pan.

Combine powdered sugar, dash of salt, and lemon juice in a small mixing bowl; beat until mixture reaches desired spreading consistency. Additional lemon juice may be added.

Spread glaze evenly over cooled mixture, and allow to set before cutting into 3- x 1½-inch bars. Yield: 1½ dozen.

The New England settlers lost little time in distilling rum. The South willingly traded tobacco for the spiritous libation, and it soon became, in the opinion of many, all too popular. "Demon rum" became the object of impassioned denunciation from colonial pulpits. The planters' morning draft, the julep, was made of rum long before corn whiskey evolved.

RASPBERRY JAM LOGS

1 cup all-purpose flour
1 teaspoon baking powder
½ cup butter or margarine, melted and slightly cooled
1 egg, beaten
1 teaspoon milk
⅓ cup raspberry jam
¼ cup butter or margarine, softened
1 cup sugar
1 egg, beaten
1 teaspoon vanilla extract
1 (7-ounce) can flaked coconut

Combine flour and baking powder in a medium mixing bowl; gradually stir in ½ cup melted butter, mixing well. Stir in 1 egg and milk.

Press mixture into a greased 12- x 8- x 2-inch baking dish. Spread jam over mixture; set aside.

Cream ¼ cup butter in a large mixing bowl; gradually add sugar, beating well. Stir in remaining egg and vanilla, mixing well. Add coconut, stir well. Spread over jam. Bake at 350° for 30 minutes. Cool and cut into 3- x 1½-inch bars. Yield: about 2 dozen.

A sprinkling of light rum adds flavor to Rum Bars. The alcohol will dissipate.

RUM BARS

4½ cups chopped pecans, divided
1 cup butter or margarine, softened
2¼ cups firmly packed brown sugar
4 eggs
2 tablespoons vanilla extract
2¼ cups all-purpose flour
2 cups candied red cherries, chopped
1½ cups chopped candied pineapple
½ cup chopped candied citron
Light rum

Sprinkle 3 cups pecans evenly over a greased 15- x 10- x 1-inch jellyroll pan; set aside.

Cream butter in a large mixing bowl; gradually add sugar, beating well. Add eggs, one at a time, beating well after each addition. Stir in vanilla. Gradually add flour, stirring well. Spoon batter into pan.

Combine cherries, pineapple, citron, and remaining pecans in a large mixing bowl; mix well. Gently press candied fruit mixture into batter. Bake at 350° for 1 hour and 15 minutes or until lightly browned. Cool slightly; cut into 2- x 1-inch bars. Sprinkle rum over each bar. Yield: about 6 dozen.

Note: Store rum bars 2 to 3 weeks in airtight containers to mellow.

A BROWNIE BY ANY OTHER NAME . . .

BROWNIES

1 cup butter or margarine, melted
¼ cup plus 2 tablespoons cocoa
2 cups sugar
4 eggs, beaten
2 cups all-purpose flour
2 teaspoons vanilla extract
2 cups chopped pecans

Combine butter and cocoa in a large mixing bowl, stirring well. Stir in sugar, eggs, flour, vanilla, and pecans. Spread batter evenly in two greased 9-inch square baking pans.

Bake at 350° for 20 to 25 minutes. Cool and cut into 1½-inch squares. Yield: about 3 dozen.

Lady Bird Johnson, wife of President Lyndon B. Johnson, shown at the family ranch in Texas.

LADY BIRD'S TEXAS BROWNIES

½ cup butter or margarine, softened
1 cup sugar
2 eggs
2 (1-ounce) squares unsweetened chocolate, melted
¾ cup all-purpose flour
1 teaspoon vanilla extract
½ cup coarsely chopped pecans

Cream butter in a large mixing bowl; gradually add sugar, beating well. Add eggs, one at a time, beating well after each addition. Add melted chocolate, and beat until blended. Gradually add flour, stirring well. Stir in vanilla and pecans. Pour batter into a greased 8-inch square baking pan.

Bake at 350° for 25 minutes. Cool brownies completely in pan. Cut into 2-inch squares. Yield: about 1½ dozen.

CHOCOLATE DREAM BROWNIES

1 cup shortening
4 (1-ounce) squares unsweetened chocolate
2 cups sugar
4 eggs, beaten
1 teaspoon vanilla extract
1½ cups all-purpose flour
½ teaspoon salt
1 cup chopped pecans
Frosting (recipe follows)
Finely chopped pecans (optional)

Combine shortening and chocolate in top of a double boiler; place over simmering water, and cook, stirring constantly, until mixture melts.

Remove from heat, and add sugar, mixing well. Add eggs and vanilla; beat until well blended. Gradually add flour and salt, stirring well after each addition. Fold in 1 cup pecans.

Spread batter evenly in a well-greased 13- x 9- x 2-inch baking pan. Bake at 400° for 20 minutes. Cool completely in pan.

Spread frosting evenly over surface of brownies, and sprinkle with finely chopped pecans, if desired. Allow frosting to set before cutting brownies into 3- x 2-inch bars or assorted shapes. Yield: about 1½ dozen.

Frosting:

2 (1-ounce) squares unsweetened chocolate
3 tablespoons water
1 tablespoon butter or margarine, softened
2 cups sifted powdered sugar
½ teaspoon vanilla extract
1 egg, beaten

Combine chocolate and water in top of a double boiler; place over simmering water and cook, stirring constantly, until chocolate melts.

Remove from heat; add butter, and stir well. Cool slightly. Gradually add remaining ingredients, beating until smooth. Use immediately. Yield: frosting for one 13- x 9-inch cake.

The Lyndon Baines Johnson Library

Chocolate Dream Brownies, viewed from different angle

FRANKLIN BROWNIES

4 (1-ounce) squares
   semisweet chocolate
1 cup butter or margarine
2 cups sugar
4 eggs
1 teaspoon vanilla extract
2 cups all-purpose flour
1 teaspoon salt
1 cup chopped pecans
Frosting (recipe follows)

Combine chocolate and butter in top of a double boiler; place over simmering water, and cook, stirring constantly, until mixture melts. Remove from heat, and cool.

Stir in sugar; add eggs, one at a time, beating well after each addition. Add vanilla, and stir until well blended.

Combine flour, salt, and pecans in a small mixing bowl; stir to coat well. Gradually add to chocolate mixture, stirring well after each addition.

Spread mixture evenly in a greased and floured 15- x 10- x 1-inch jellyroll pan. Bake at 325° for 30 minutes. Remove from oven, and cool completely in pan. Spread frosting evenly over brownies, and allow to set before cutting into 2-inch squares. Yield: about 3 dozen.

Frosting:

1½ cups sugar
2 (1-ounce) squares
   semisweet chocolate
½ cup butter or margarine
½ cup milk
1 teaspoon vanilla extract

Combine all ingredients, except vanilla, in a large saucepan; bring to a rolling boil, stirring occasionally. Boil rapidly 1 minute; remove from heat, and cool slightly.

Add vanilla, and beat constantly with a wire whisk until mixture begins to thicken. Use immediately. Yield: frosting for one 15- x 10-inch cake.

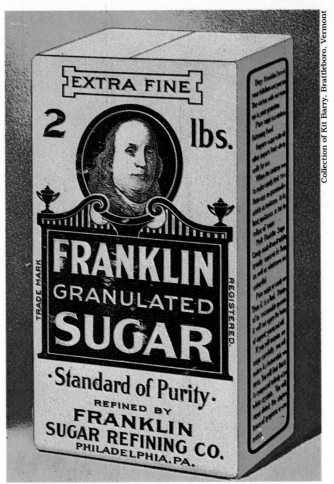

A sugar refinery cashed in on Benjamin Franklin.

CHOCOLATE SYRUP BROWNIES

½ cup butter or margarine,
   softened
1 cup sugar
4 eggs
1 (16-ounce) can chocolate
   syrup
1 cup all-purpose flour
1 cup chopped pecans
Frosting (recipe follows)

Cream butter in a large mixing bowl; gradually add sugar, beating well. Add eggs, one at a time, beating well after each addition. Add chocolate syrup; beat until well blended. Stir in flour and pecans.

Pour batter into a well-greased 15- x 10- x 1-inch jellyroll pan. Bake at 350° for 25 minutes or until a wooden pick inserted in center comes out clean. Cool completely in pan.

Spread frosting evenly over brownies. Cut into 2½-inch squares. Yield: 2 dozen.

Frosting:

1½ cups sugar
¼ cup plus 2 tablespoons
   milk
¼ cup plus 2 tablespoons
   butter or margarine, melted
1 (6-ounce) package
   semisweet chocolate
   morsels

Combine first 3 ingredients in a medium saucepan; bring to a boil, stirring constantly. Boil 1 minute. Remove from heat; stir in chocolate morsels, beating until morsels melt and mixture is of spreading consistency. Yield: frosting for one 15- x 10-inch cake.

CHOCOLATE-CARAMEL FINGERS

2 cups all-purpose flour
1 teaspoon baking powder
½ teaspoon baking soda
½ teaspoon salt
1 cup butter or margarine
2 cups firmly packed dark brown sugar
2 eggs, lightly beaten
1 (6-ounce) package semisweet chocolate morsels
Sifted powdered sugar

Sift together flour, baking powder, soda, and salt in a small mixing bowl; set aside.

Melt butter in a large saucepan over medium heat. Remove from heat. Add brown sugar, eggs, reserved flour mixture, and chocolate morsels, stirring well after each addition until thoroughly blended.

Pour batter into a lightly greased and floured 15- x 10- x 1-inch jellyroll pan. Bake at 325° for 25 minutes or until a wooden pick inserted in center comes out clean; sprinkle with powdered sugar. Cool completely in pan; cut into 3- x 1-inch bars to serve. Yield: about 4 dozen.

A s widespread as chocoholism is in this country, we are moderates in comparison with the Swiss; they eat twice as many pounds per capita each year. All chocolate stems from within 20 degrees of the equator, with most coming from Bahia in Brazil. Long after chocolate became a beverage in England and America, the Swiss developed machinery for making solid milk chocolate in 1875. Machines that stirred liquid chocolate enhanced its smoothness for eating and cooking.

GERMAN CHOCOLATE BROWNIES

1 (4-ounce) package sweet baking chocolate
2 eggs, lightly beaten
1 cup sugar
¾ cup all-purpose flour
¾ cup chopped pecans
½ cup butter or margarine, melted
1 teaspoon vanilla extract
Frosting (recipe follows)

Melt chocolate in top of a double boiler over simmering water. Remove from heat, and cool slightly. Set aside.

Combine eggs and sugar in a medium mixing bowl; beat with a wire whisk until well blended. Add reserved chocolate, flour, pecans, butter, and vanilla; beat with a wire whisk until well blended.

Pour batter into a greased 9-inch square baking pan. Bake at 350° for 40 minutes. Cool in pan on a wire rack. Spread frosting evenly over brownies, and cut into 1½-inch squares. Yield: about 3 dozen.

Frosting:

½ cup evaporated milk
½ cup sugar
¼ cup butter or margarine
2 egg yolks, lightly beaten
½ teaspoon vanilla
⅓ cup flaked coconut
½ cup chopped pecans

Combine milk, sugar, butter, and egg yolks in a medium saucepan; cook over medium heat, stirring constantly, until thickened. Remove from heat, and stir in vanilla, coconut, and pecans. Let cool completely. Yield: frosting for one 9-inch square cake.

Maillard's chocolate and cocoa trade card, c.1890.

GERMAN CREAM CHEESE BROWNIES

1 (4-ounce) package sweet baking chocolate
¼ cup plus 1 tablespoon butter, divided and softened
3 eggs
1 cup sugar, divided
1½ teaspoons vanilla extract, divided
¼ teaspoon almond extract
½ cup plus 1 tablespoon all-purpose flour, divided
½ teaspoon baking powder
¼ teaspoon salt
½ cup coarsely chopped pecans
1 (3-ounce) package cream cheese, softened

Combine chocolate and 3 tablespoons butter in top of a double boiler; place over simmering water and cook, stirring constantly, until chocolate and butter melt. Cool and set aside.

Beat 2 eggs in a medium mixing bowl; gradually add ¾ cup sugar, beating until thick and lemon colored. Add 1 teaspoon vanilla and almond extract, stirring well.

Combine ½ cup flour, baking powder, and salt in a small mixing bowl; gradually add to egg mixture, stirring well. Stir in reserved chocolate mixture and pecans.

Pour batter into a well-greased 9-inch square baking pan, reserving 1 cup batter. Set aside.

Cream remaining 2 tablespoons butter and cream cheese in a small mixing bowl; gradually add remaining ¼ cup sugar, beating until light and fluffy. Add 1 egg; beat well. Add remaining flour and vanilla, stirring well; pour evenly over chocolate batter in pan.

Drop reserved 1 cup chocolate batter by tablespoonfuls onto light-colored batter; swirl to marble. Bake at 350° for 45 minutes or until lightly browned. Cool brownies completely in pan. Cut into 1½-inch squares. Yield: about 3 dozen.

HEAVENLY FUDGE BARS

⅓ cup butter or margarine, softened
¾ cup sugar
2 eggs
1 teaspoon vanilla extract
¾ cup all-purpose flour
3 tablespoons cocoa
½ teaspoon baking soda
¼ teaspoon salt
½ cup chopped walnuts
Miniature marshmallows
Frosting (recipe follows)

Cream butter in a large mixing bowl; gradually add sugar, beating well. Add eggs, one at a time, beating well after each addition. Stir in vanilla.

Sift together flour, cocoa, soda, and salt in a medium mixing bowl; add to creamed mixture, stirring until well blended. Stir in walnuts. Pour batter into a well-greased 9-inch square baking pan.

Bake at 350° for 20 minutes. Remove from oven; top with marshmallows. Return to oven; bake an additional 5 minutes. Cool completely in pan. Spread with frosting. Cut into 2- x 1-inch bars. Yield: 3 dozen.

Frosting:

½ cup firmly packed brown sugar
2 tablespoons cocoa
¼ cup water
1½ cups sifted powdered sugar
3 tablespoons butter or margarine
1 teaspoon vanilla extract

Combine brown sugar, cocoa, and water in a medium saucepan; bring to a boil, stirring constantly. Boil 2 minutes. Remove from heat; stir in remaining ingredients. Beat until mixture is of spreading consistency. Yield: frosting for one 9-inch square cake.

Baker's Cocoa, "pure" with "no chemicals," from a Walter Baker Co. booklet, 1914,

BAKER'S BREAKFAST COCOA

LA BELLE CHOCOLATIÈRE

Walter Baker & Co., Limited
Registered in U.S. Patent Office.

Young girls, aproned and capped, in a turn-of-the-century cooking class.

CHOCOLATE CHIP BROWNIES

1 cup butter or margarine, melted
½ cup sugar
½ cup firmly packed brown sugar
2 eggs
1 teaspoon vanilla extract
2¼ cups all-purpose flour
1 teaspoon baking soda
¾ teaspoon salt
1 (12-ounce) package semisweet chocolate morsels

Combine butter and sugar in a large mixing bowl; beat well. Add eggs and vanilla, beating well. Combine flour, soda, and salt. Add to creamed mixture; mix well. Add chocolate morsels, stirring well.

Spread batter evenly in an ungreased 13- x 9- x 2-inch baking pan. Bake at 350° for 20 to 25 minutes. Cut into 2-inch squares while warm. Cool completely, and serve. Yield: about 2 dozen.

DELTA BARS

½ cup shortening
1 cup sugar
1 egg
1 egg, separated
1 teaspoon vanilla extract
1¼ cups all-purpose flour
1 teaspoon baking powder
½ teaspoon salt
1 cup firmly packed brown sugar
½ cup semisweet chocolate morsels
½ cup chopped pecans

Cream shortening in a large mixing bowl; gradually add 1 cup sugar, beating well. Add 1 egg and egg yolk to creamed mixture; beat well. Add vanilla, and stir well.

Combine flour, baking powder, and salt in a small mixing bowl; add to creamed mixture, stirring until smooth. Press mixture evenly into a greased 13- x 9- x 2-inch baking pan, and set aside.

Beat egg white (at room temperature) until foamy; gradually add brown sugar, 1 tablespoon at a time, beating until stiff peaks form. Fold in chocolate morsels and pecans. Spread evenly over mixture in pan. Bake at 375° for 25 minutes; cool completely, and cut into 3- x 1-inch bars. Yield: about 3 dozen.

TOFFEE BARS

1 cup butter, softened
1 cup firmly packed
  brown sugar
1 teaspoon vanilla extract
2 cups all-purpose flour
1 (6-ounce) package
  semisweet chocolate
  morsels
1 cup chopped pecans

Cream butter in a large mixing bowl; gradually add sugar and vanilla, beating until light and fluffy. Stir in flour, chocolate morsels, and pecans.

Press dough evenly into an ungreased 15- x 10- x 1-inch jelly-roll pan. Bake at 350° for 25 to 30 minutes. Cut into 3- x 1-inch bars while warm. Cool completely in pan. Yield: about 4 dozen.

Toffee Bars, natural go-withs for tea, coffee, or milk.

BROWNIE GRAHAMS

2 cups graham cracker
  crumbs
1 (6-ounce) package
  semisweet chocolate
  morsels
½ cup coarsely chopped
  pecans
1 (14-ounce) can sweetened
  condensed milk

Combine cracker crumbs, chocolate morsels, and pecans in a large mixing bowl; stir well. Add condensed milk, and stir until well blended.

Press mixture evenly into a well-greased 8-inch square baking pan. Bake at 350° for 30 minutes. Cool completely in pan; cut into 2-inch squares. Yield: about 1½ dozen.

PEANUT BROWNIES

½ cup shortening
1 cup all-purpose flour
½ teaspoon baking powder
½ teaspoon salt
1½ cups sugar
3 eggs
½ cup smooth peanut
  butter
1 teaspoon vanilla extract
1 (6-ounce) package
  semisweet chocolate
  morsels
1 cup chopped peanuts

Melt shortening in a small saucepan over low heat; remove from heat, and set aside to cool slightly.

Combine flour, baking powder, and salt in a small mixing bowl; stir well, and set aside.

Combine melted shortening and sugar in a large mixing bowl; beat until well blended. Add eggs, peanut butter, and vanilla, beating well. Gradually add reserved flour mixture to peanut butter mixture, stirring well after each addition. Fold in chocolate morsels and peanuts.

Spread mixture evenly in a well-greased 13- x 9- x 2-inch baking pan. Bake at 350° for 35 minutes. Cool completely in pan; cut into 3- x 1½-inch bars. Yield: about 2 dozen.

Inspecting peanuts at the Beech Nut plant, 1927.

PEANUT BUTTER SQUARES

½ cup smooth peanut butter
⅓ cup butter or margarine, softened
1 cup sugar
¼ cup firmly packed brown sugar
2 eggs
½ teaspoon vanilla extract
1 cup all-purpose flour
1 teaspoon baking powder
¼ teaspoon salt
1 (6-ounce) package semisweet chocolate morsels

Combine peanut butter and butter in a large mixing bowl; beat well. Gradually add sugar, beating well. Add eggs, beating well. Stir in vanilla.

Combine flour, baking powder, and salt in a small mixing bowl; gradually add to peanut butter mixture, stirring well after each addition. Fold in chocolate morsels.

Spoon mixture into a well-greased 9-inch square baking pan. Bake at 350° for 30 minutes. Cool completely in pan; cut into 1½-inch squares. Yield: about 3 dozen.

APRICOT BLONDIES

½ cup shortening
1 cup firmly packed brown sugar
2 eggs
1½ teaspoons vanilla extract
1¾ cups all-purpose flour
2 teaspoons baking powder
½ teaspoon salt
1 cup chopped dried apricots
½ cup chopped pecans

Combine shortening and sugar; beat well. Add eggs, one at a time, beating well after each addition. Stir in vanilla. Combine flour, baking powder, and salt; add to creamed mixture, mixing well. Fold in apricots and pecans.

Press mixture evenly into a greased 13- x 9- x 2-inch baking pan. Bake at 350° for 18 to 20 minutes. Cool completely, and cut into 2- x 1-inch bars. Yield: about 4½ dozen.

CHEWY BLONDE BROWNIES

¼ cup butter or margarine, melted
1 cup firmly packed brown sugar
1 egg
1 teaspoon vanilla extract
1 cup all-purpose flour
¼ teaspoon baking soda
¼ teaspoon salt
½ cup chopped pecans

Combine butter and brown sugar in a large mixing bowl, mixing well. Add egg and vanilla, beating well.

Sift together flour, soda, and salt in a small mixing bowl. Gradually add to creamed mixture, stirring well. Stir in pecans. Spread mixture in a greased 9-inch square baking pan. Bake at 350° for 25 minutes. Cool and cut into 1½-inch squares. Yield: 3 dozen.

SHEFFIELD CHEWS

½ cup butter or margarine,
  melted
1 cup sugar
1 egg
1 egg, separated
1¼ cups all-purpose flour
1 teaspoon baking powder
Dash of salt
2 teaspoons vanilla extract,
  divided
¾ cup firmly packed
  brown sugar
1 cup chopped pecans

Combine butter and 1 cup sugar in a medium mixing bowl, stirring until well blended. Add 1 egg and egg yolk; mix well.

Combine flour, baking powder, and salt; add to butter mixture, mixing well. Stir in 1 teaspoon vanilla. Spread mixture evenly in a greased 13- x 9- x 2-inch baking pan; set aside.

Lightly beat 1 egg white (at room temperature); gradually add brown sugar, beating well. Stir in pecans and remaining vanilla. Spread pecan mixture evenly over prepared crust. Bake at 375° for 15 minutes; reduce temperature to 325°, and bake 20 minutes. Cool completely in pan on a wire rack, and cut into 2-inch squares. Yield: about 2 dozen.

BUTTER CHEWS

1 cup all-purpose flour
¼ cup sifted powdered sugar
½ cup butter, softened
3 eggs, separated
¾ cup firmly packed
  brown sugar
¾ cup flaked coconut
1 cup chopped pecans

Combine flour and powdered sugar in a small mixing bowl; stir well. Cut in butter with a pastry blender until mixture resembles coarse meal. Press firmly into a lightly greased 9-inch square baking pan. Bake at 350° for 15 minutes. Remove from oven, and set aside.

Beat egg yolks in a large mixing bowl; add remaining ingredients, stirring well.

Beat egg whites (at room temperature) in a medium mixing bowl until stiff peaks form. Fold into egg yolk mixture. Pour over reserved hot crust. Bake at 350° for 30 minutes or until browned. Cut into 1-inch squares while warm. Yield: about 7 dozen.

WAX COOKIES

¾ cup butter or margarine
2 cups firmly packed
  brown sugar
4 eggs, lightly beaten
1 teaspoon vanilla extract
1½ cups all-purpose flour
½ teaspoon baking powder
Dash of salt
1 cup chopped pecans

Melt butter in a heavy saucepan; add sugar, stirring until well blended. Bring to a boil over medium heat, stirring constantly. Remove from heat, and cool slightly. Add eggs, one at a time, beating well after each addition. Stir in vanilla.

Combine flour, baking powder, and salt in a small mixing bowl; add to sugar mixture, stirring well. Stir in pecans. Pour batter into a greased 13- x 9- x 2-inch baking pan. Bake at 350° for 25 to 30 minutes. Cool completely, and cut into 2-inch squares. Yield: about 2 dozen.

For Wax Cookies, batter is quickly mixed in a saucepan.

For Southern hostesses, education has always begun at home. Photograph c.189

BAKE AND CELEBRATE

"Every Christmas collection of cookies should contain a few of these delicious cinnamon-almond stars," according to Marion Flexner, the Alabama-born author of *Out of Kentucky Kitchens*. She was referring to Zimtsterne, a holiday tradition brought by German immigrants to the South. Lebkuchen, Springerle . . . an entire region shares in the baking genius of those Germans who overcame such odds to become Texans in the 1800s. "Christmas isn't complete without our Half-Moons," they say down around Castroville, where more Alsatians settled.

Gingerbread men are of the old "add-flour-to-roll" school we can trace back to the English of the Eastern Seaboard. So too are butter cookies, perfect for Valentine hearts and other shapings and small fruit "cakes."

Hallmarks of much Greek-American holiday baking are honey, nuts, and spice, but New Year's calls for cookies full of real butter, heaped high in such a cloud of powdered sugar that the uninitiated must beware inhaling it. For Easter, Greek cookies take on round and twisted shapes that carry religious significance.

By 1880, there were 880 Norwegian settlers in Texas, mostly in Bosque County. They brought krumkake and rosette irons with them, along with a treasury of holiday cookies to add to those already in the South.

A cautionary note comes with the recipe for Bizcochos: "Make them with lard or they aren't authentic!" These choice cookies go well with the old Mexican Christmas custom of Las Posadas (The Inns) in which carolers portray the Holy Family in search of lodging. They are turned away from every door until, at the last house, they are invited in for a joyous sharing of Bizcochos and Mexican chocolate.

Chanukah commemorates a miracle recorded in Jewish history in which a one-day supply of oil lasted eight days, the amount of days needed to replenish a supply destroyed by enemies of the faith. The eight-branched Menorah is brought out, and one candle is lighted the first evening, and so on, until, on the eighth night, all candles are ablaze. Children anticipate eight full days of feasting, so no Jewish mother would enter into Chanukah without a week-long baking spree. Symbol Cookies will be among those treats.

Holidays bring out the best of Southern cookie baking. For Christmas or Chanukah we may splurge the most, but we don't neglect Saints Valentine and Patrick. Shown: Zimtkränze (front), Fruit-Shaped Butter cookies, and chunky Lizzies (rear).

ALMOND CHRISTMAS COOKIES

3 cups all-purpose flour
1¼ cups sugar, divided
1½ cups butter, softened
1 egg
1 egg, well beaten
Sliced almonds
1 tablespoon ground
  cinnamon

Sift together flour and 1 cup sugar in a large mixing bowl; cut in butter with a pastry blender until mixture resembles coarse meal. Turn dough out, and knead 4 to 5 times on a well-floured surface, and return dough to mixing bowl. Add 1 egg, using hands to mix well. Repeat kneading procedure.

Divide dough into fourths, and chill 2 hours. Roll one portion of dough to ¼-inch thickness on a lightly floured surface; keep remaining dough chilled until ready to use. Cut with a 2-inch round cutter.

Place on greased cookie sheets; brush with beaten egg. Press 3 almond slices in center of each cookie to resemble flower petals. Combine remaining ¼ cup sugar and cinnamon; sprinkle over cookies.

Bake at 350° for 8 minutes or until lightly browned. Remove from cookie sheets, and cool on wire racks. Repeat procedure with remaining dough. Yield: about 6½ dozen.

A Royal Granite Steel Ware advertisement conjures a raucous Christmas morning scene back in 1911.

AMBROSIA COOKIES

1 cup butter or margarine,
  softened
1 cup sugar
1 cup firmly packed
  brown sugar
2 eggs
1 teaspoon vanilla extract
2 cups all-purpose flour
1 teaspoon baking powder
½ teaspoon baking soda
½ teaspoon salt
1½ cups quick-cooking
  oats, uncooked
1 teaspoon grated orange rind
1 teaspoon grated lemon rind
1 cup chopped dates
1 cup golden raisins
1 cup flaked coconut
1 cup chopped pecans

Cream butter in a large mixing bowl; gradually add sugar, beating well. Add eggs, one at a time, beating well after each addition. Stir in vanilla.

Combine flour, baking powder, soda, and salt in a medium mixing bowl; add to creamed mixture, stirring well. Stir in remaining ingredients.

Drop by teaspoonfuls 2 inches apart onto lightly greased cookie sheets. Bake at 375° for 8 to 10 minutes. Remove from cookie sheets; cool on wire racks. Yield: about 5 dozen.

Note: Store cookies in airtight containers for several days to improve flavor.

When the Royal Boy enters the home he brings happiness.

AIKEN'S ROW BOURBON COOKIES

½ cup butter or margarine, softened
1 cup firmly packed brown sugar
4 eggs
1 tablespoon baking soda
1 tablespoon milk
3 cups all-purpose flour
1 teaspoon ground cinnamon
1 teaspoon ground nutmeg
⅔ cup bourbon
5 cups chopped pecans
3 cups raisins
3 cups candied red cherries, chopped
1½ cups candied red pineapple, chopped
1½ cups candied green pineapple, chopped
1 (7-ounce) can flaked coconut
1½ tablespoons grated orange rind

Cream butter in a large mixing bowl; gradually add sugar, beating well. Add eggs, one at a time, beating well after each addition. Dissolve soda in milk; stir into creamed mixture.

Sift together flour, cinnamon, and nutmeg in a medium mixing bowl. Add to creamed mixture alternately with bourbon, beginning and ending with flour mixture. Stir well after each addition. Stir in remaining ingredients; mix well.

Drop dough by teaspoonfuls 2 inches apart onto greased cookie sheets. Bake at 300° for 25 minutes or until lightly browned. Remove from cookie sheets, and cool on wire racks. Yield: about 10 dozen.

Superior Bourbon Whiskey label, 1875. True bourbon is distilled from a mash with at least 51% corn.

When Governor William Aiken began development of Aiken's Row in 1845, he started with one house on the corner, his own, then added the remaining seven. His home was profligately furnished, and his detractors called the additional houses "the seven days of the week" because their rent paid for his extravagance. The Row was in a suburb of Charleston called Wraggbrough, on Wragg Square, looking down an avenue of stately oaks. Long since engulfed by the city of Charleston, Aiken's Row now has only two of the original seven buildings remaining, and only one remains as a private domicile.

SUPERIOR BOURBON WHISKEY.

OLD EXTRA FINE

This Christmas party displays a forest of Christmas trees and features Santa, 1900.

CHRISTMAS BUTTER COOKIES

¾ cup butter
¼ cup sugar
⅔ cup ground almonds
2 teaspoons cold water
2 teaspoons vanilla extract
1¾ cups all-purpose flour
Dash of salt
Sifted powdered sugar

Cream butter in a medium mixing bowl; gradually add ¼ cup sugar, beating until light and fluffy. Add almonds, water, and vanilla; beat well. Stir in flour and salt; mix well.

Shape 1 teaspoon dough into a 2-inch finger. Repeat procedure with remaining dough. Place 1 inch apart on ungreased cookie sheets. Bake at 300° for 25 to 30 minutes. Remove cookies to wire racks to cool. Roll cookies in powdered sugar. Yield: about 4½ dozen.

Snowy Christmas Butter Cookies, Chocolate-Walnut Christmas Cookies, and Cherry Delights all say "Happy Holidays!"

CHOCOLATE-WALNUT CHRISTMAS COOKIES

½ cup butter or margarine, softened
1 cup firmly packed brown sugar
1 egg
1 teaspoon vanilla extract
2 (1-ounce) squares unsweetened chocolate, melted
1½ cups all-purpose flour
1 teaspoon baking powder
½ teaspoon baking soda
1 cup chopped black walnuts

Cream butter in a large mixing bowl; gradually add sugar, beating well. Add egg and vanilla; beat well. Add melted chocolate, beating until smooth.

Combine flour, baking powder, and soda in a medium mixing bowl; add to creamed mixture, stirring well. Stir in walnuts.

Drop by heaping teaspoonfuls 2 inches apart onto greased cookie sheets. Bake at 375° for 8 to 10 minutes. Remove from cookie sheets; cool on wire racks. Yield: 3½ dozen.

CHERRY DELIGHTS

1 cup butter or margarine, softened
½ cup sugar
½ cup light corn syrup
2 eggs, separated
2½ cups all-purpose flour
2 cups finely chopped pecans
Candied red cherries, halved

Cream butter in a large mixing bowl. Add sugar, syrup, and egg yolks; beat well. Gradually add flour, stirring well.

Shape dough into 1-inch balls. Dip each ball into lightly beaten egg whites; roll in pecans, coating well.

Place 2 inches apart on lightly greased cookie sheets. Press a cherry half into center of each cookie. Bake at 325° for 20 to 25 minutes. Cool slightly on cookie sheets. Remove to wire racks to cool completely. Yield: 4½ dozen.

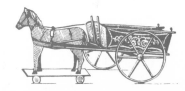

CHERRY WINKS

¾ cup butter
1 cup sugar
2 eggs
2 tablespoons milk
1 teaspoon vanilla extract
2¼ cups all-purpose flour
1 teaspoon baking
  powder
½ teaspoon baking soda
½ teaspoon salt
1 cup chopped pecans
1 cup chopped dates
⅓ cup drained and chopped
  maraschino cherries
2½ cups crushed corn flakes
  cereal
Additional maraschino
  cherries, drained and cut
  into quarters

Cream butter in a large mixing bowl; gradually add sugar, beating until light and fluffy. Add eggs, milk, and vanilla, beating well.

Combine flour, baking powder, soda, and salt in a medium mixing bowl; sift 3 times. Add to creamed mixture, stirring well; stir in pecans, dates, and chopped cherries, mixing well. Cover and refrigerate overnight.

Shape dough into 1-inch balls, and roll in crushed cereal. Place 2 inches apart on lightly greased cookie sheets; flatten each ball slightly with the bottom of a glass. Place a cherry quarter on top of each cookie. Bake at 375° for 8 to 10 minutes or until lightly browned. Remove from cookie sheets, and cool on wire racks. Yield: about 7 dozen.

Cherry Winks will be recognized by those who were baking or eating cookies in the early 1950s. The recipe won the $5,000 first prize, Junior Division, in the Second Grand National Recipe and Baking Contest, as the Pillsbury Bake-Off® was first called. Starlight Mint Surprise Cookies (page 82) took the $10,000 second prize in the first contest in 1949, and Peanut Blossoms (page 81) was a finalist in 1957. Phillip Pillsbury conceived the idea for the Bake-Off® and attended every one of them until his death in 1984. He made a point of meeting each contestant and proudly led the Grand March of one-hundred finalists. An amazing number of our good recipes are Pillsbury finds.

CHRISTMAS FRUIT COOKIES

2 (8-ounce) packages pitted
    dates, chopped
2½ cups chopped candied
    red cherries
½ cup chopped candied
    citron (optional)
3 cups all-purpose flour,
    divided
4 cups chopped walnuts
¼ teaspoon baking soda
2 tablespoons water
1 cup butter or margarine,
    softened
2½ cups sugar
4 eggs
1 teaspoon baking powder
Dash of salt
1 teaspoon vanilla extract

Combine dates, cherries, and
citron, if desired, in a large mixing bowl; add 1 cup flour, stirring to coat well. Add walnuts,
stirring well; set aside.

Combine soda and water, stirring well; set aside.

Cream butter in a large mixing bowl; gradually add sugar,
beating well. Add eggs, one at a
time, beating well after each addition.

Sift together remaining flour,
baking powder, and salt in a
medium mixing bowl. Add to
creamed mixture; stir well. Add
dissolved soda and vanilla, stirring well. Stir in reserved fruit
mixture.

Drop dough by heaping teaspoonfuls 2 inches apart onto
greased cookie sheets. Bake at
275° for 30 minutes or until
lightly browned. Remove from
cookie sheets, and cool on wire
racks. Store in airtight containers. Yield: about 20 dozen.

Collection of Business Americana

Die-cut of a beautifully adorned Christmas tree, c.1890.

FRUITCAKE COOKIES

3 cups chopped pecans
1 (8-ounce) package chopped
    dates
1 (8-ounce) package candied
    pineapple, chopped
1 (4-ounce) package candied
    red cherries, chopped
1 (4-ounce) package candied
    green cherries, chopped
2 cups all-purpose flour,
    divided
½ cup butter or margarine,
    softened
1 cup firmly packed
    brown sugar
2 eggs
1 teaspoon baking soda
2 tablespoons buttermilk
½ teaspoon ground
    cinnamon
½ teaspoon ground allspice
½ teaspoon ground nutmeg
2 tablespoons rum or wine

Combine first 5 ingredients in
a large mixing bowl; add 1 cup
flour, stirring to coat well. Set
aside.

Cream butter in a large mixing bowl; gradually add sugar,
beating well. Add eggs, beating
until well blended.

Dissolve soda in buttermilk.
Combine remaining flour, cinnamon, allspice, and nutmeg.
Add to creamed mixture alternately with buttermilk mixture
and rum, beginning and ending
with flour mixture. Stir in fruit
mixture.

Drop by heaping teaspoonfuls
2 inches apart onto lightly
greased cookie sheets. Bake at
325° for 12 minutes or until
lightly browned. Remove from
cookie sheets, and cool on wire
racks. Yield: 9 dozen.

Fanciful creatures find a wealth of mincemeat in this Armour and Company trade card, c.1895.

LIZZIES

3 cups golden raisins
½ cup bourbon
½ cup butter or margarine, softened
½ cup firmly packed brown sugar
2 eggs
1½ cups all-purpose flour
1½ teaspoons baking soda
1½ teaspoons ground cinnamon
½ teaspoon ground nutmeg
½ teaspoon ground cloves
2 (8-ounce) packages chopped candied red cherries
2 (4-ounce) packages chopped candied citron
4 cups pecan halves

Combine raisins and bourbon in a medium mixing bowl, stirring well; let stand 1 hour.

Cream butter in a large mixing bowl; gradually add sugar, beating until light and fluffy. Add eggs; beating until well blended.

Sift together flour, soda, cinnamon, nutmeg, and cloves; add to creamed mixture, stirring well. Stir in cherries, citron, reserved raisins, and pecan halves.

Drop by tablespoonfuls 2 inches apart onto greased cookie sheets. Bake at 325° for 15 minutes. Cool slightly on cookie sheets. Remove to wire racks to cool completely. Yield: 13½ dozen.

MINCEMEAT DROPS

⅓ cup shortening
½ cup sugar
1 egg, beaten
1½ cups all-purpose flour
½ teaspoon baking soda
¼ teaspoon salt
¾ cup prepared mincemeat
¼ teaspoon vanilla extract

Cream shortening in a medium mixing bowl; gradually add sugar, beating until light and fluffy. Add beaten egg, beating well. Combine flour, soda, and salt in a small mixing bowl; add to creamed mixture, stirring well. Stir in mincemeat and vanilla.

Drop dough by teaspoonfuls 2 inches apart onto greased cookie sheets. Bake at 375° for 10 to 12 minutes. Cool slightly on cookie sheets. Remove to wire racks to cool completely. Yield: 3½ dozen.

ORANGE-MINCEMEAT FILLED COOKIES

½ cup shortening
¾ cup sugar
2 eggs
1 tablespoon grated
  orange rind
½ teaspoon frozen orange
  juice concentrate, thawed
2 cups all-purpose flour
2 teaspoons baking powder
1 teaspoon salt
About ⅔ cup mincemeat

Cream shortening in a large mixing bowl; gradually add sugar, beating well. Add eggs, beating until well blended. Stir in orange rind and juice.

Sift together flour, baking powder, and salt in a medium mixing bowl; gradually add to orange mixture, stirring until well blended. Divide dough in half; cover and refrigerate 2 hours.

Roll one half of dough to ¼-inch thickness on a floured surface, keeping remaining half chilled until ready to use; cut into 3-inch squares. Place a heaping teaspoon of mincemeat in center of each square. Moisten edges with water; fold pastry in half. Press pastry edges firmly together with tines of a fork.

Place on greased cookies sheets, and bake at 375° for 8 to 10 minutes. Cool slightly on cookie sheets. Remove to wire racks to cool completely. Repeat procedure with remaining dough and mincemeat. Yield: 2½ dozen.

Saying Grace at a children's Christmas dinner party. An 1890s stereograph card.

BRANDIED FRUIT LOGS

1½ cups currants
1½ cups raisins
1½ cups candied red
  cherries, halved
1½ cups chopped candied
  pineapple
1½ cups brandy
½ cup butter or margarine,
  softened
1½ cups firmly packed
  brown sugar
3 eggs
2 cups all-purpose flour
½ teaspoon baking soda
½ teaspoon salt
1 teaspoon ground cinnamon
1 teaspoon ground allspice
1 teaspoon ground cloves
Dash of ground nutmeg

Combine currants, raisins, and candied fruit in a large mixing bowl; add brandy, and stir well. Cover tightly, and let stand at room temperature 1 to 2 days, stirring occasionally.

Cream butter in a large mixing bowl; add sugar, and beat well. Add eggs, one at a time, beating well after each addition.

Sift together flour, soda, salt, cinnamon, allspice, cloves, and nutmeg in a medium mixing bowl. Gradually add to creamed mixture, stirring well after each addition. Fold in reserved brandied fruit mixture.

Spread mixture evenly in a greased 15- x 10- x 1-inch jellyroll pan. Bake at 325° for 35 minutes. Cool completely in pan before cutting into 3- x 1½-inch bars. Yield: about 2½ dozen.

GUMDROP COOKIES

2 cups firmly packed
  brown sugar
4 eggs, separated
2 cups all-purpose flour
¼ teaspoon salt
1 teaspoon ground cinnamon
2 tablespoons water
1 cup assorted miniature,
  colored gumdrops, chopped
1 cup chopped pecans
2 cups sifted powdered sugar
¼ cup butter or margarine,
  melted
2 teaspoons grated orange
  rind
¼ cup orange juice

Combine brown sugar and egg yolks in a large mixing bowl; beat until well blended. Sift together flour, salt, and cinnamon in a small mixing bowl. Gradually add two-thirds of flour mixture to creamed mixture alternately with water, beginning and ending with flour mixture. Stir well after each addition. Add chopped gumdrops and pecans to remaining flour mixture; stir to coat well, and set aside.

Beat egg whites (at room temperature) in a small mixing bowl until stiff peaks form. Fold into batter alternately with reserved gumdrop mixture.

Spread mixture evenly in a greased 15- x 10- x 1-inch jellyroll pan. Bake at 350° for 20 minutes or until a wooden pick inserted in center comes out clean. Set aside to cool in pan.

Combine remaining ingredients in a small mixing bowl; beat until well blended. Spread evenly over cookies in pan. Allow glaze to set before cutting into 3- x 1-inch bars. Yield: about 4 dozen.

CHERRY-COCONUT BARS

½ cup butter or margarine,
  softened
1¼ cups all-purpose flour,
  divided
3 tablespoons sifted
  powdered sugar
2 eggs
1 cup sugar
½ teaspoon baking powder
¼ teaspoon salt
1 teaspoon vanilla extract
½ cup flaked coconut
½ cup drained and chopped
  maraschino cherries
¾ cup chopped pecans

Cream butter in a medium mixing bowl; gradually add 1 cup flour and powdered sugar, beating well. Press mixture evenly into a lightly greased 8-inch square baking pan. Bake at 350° for 20 minutes or until lightly browned.

Beat eggs in a medium mixing bowl until foamy; add 1 cup sugar, remaining flour, baking powder, salt, vanilla, coconut, cherries, and pecans, mixing well. Spread evenly over baked pastry. Bake at 350° for 20 minutes. Cool completely in pan. Cut into 2- x 1-inch bars to serve. Yield: about 2½ dozen.

OLD-WORLD TRADITIONS

SPECULAAS

1 cup butter, softened
1 cup firmly packed
  brown sugar
2 tablespoons milk
2 teaspoons grated
  orange rind
2 cups all-purpose flour
1 tablespoon baking powder
½ teaspoon salt
1 tablespoon ground
  cinnamon
1 teaspoon grated nutmeg
½ teaspoon ground cloves
½ teaspoon pepper
½ teaspoon anise seeds,
  crushed
½ cup blanched whole
  almonds

Cream butter in a large mixing bowl; add sugar, and beat until light and fluffy. Add milk and orange rind; beat until well blended.

Sift together remaining ingredients, except almonds, in a medium mixing bowl. Gradually add to creamed mixture, beating well. (Use additional milk, if necessary.)

Divide dough in half; press each portion to ½-inch thickness on a greased cookie sheet. Cut each portion into 10 rectangles, and press 4 almonds into each rectangle. (Wooden cookie molds may be used to press dough into assorted shapes, omitting almonds.)

Preheat oven to 425° for 7 minutes; reduce heat to 325°, and bake cookies for 25 minutes. Cool slightly on cookie sheets. Remove to wire racks to cool completely. Break cookies apart, and store in airtight containers. Yield: about 2 dozen.

Speculaas are part of the Dutch tradition of St. Nicholas Day, celebrated December 5 in Holland. The night before, children leave carrots in their shoes for the Saint's horse; in the morning, each child finds treats in place of the carrot. At evening appear the larger gifts, but at the end of a treasure hunt. Speculaas, baked in people-shaped molds called bachelors and spinsters, are given to single friends.

Children attend a costume celebration with a Dutch flair. Photograph c.1920, Richmond, Virginia.

GREEK HOLIDAY COOKIES

2 cups all-purpose flour
½ teaspoon salt
¾ cup shortening
5 to 6 tablespoons cold water
1 (6-ounce) jar maraschino
  cherries, undrained
1 cup chopped pecans
¼ cup quince jelly
¼ teaspoon ground
  cinnamon
1½ teaspoons Cognac
Maraschino cherry halves,
  drained
½ cup sugar
1 cup water
2 tablespoons honey
1½ teaspoons lemon juice

Combine flour and salt in a medium mixing bowl; cut in shortening with a pastry blender until mixture resembles coarse meal. Sprinkle 5 to 6 tablespoons water evenly over surface of flour mixture; stir with a fork until dry ingredients are moistened. Shape dough into a ball; chill.

Drain cherries, reserving liquid; chop cherries. Combine cherries, reserved liquid, pecans, jelly, cinnamon, and Cognac in a medium mixing bowl; mix until thoroughly blended. Set aside.

Roll half of pastry to ⅛-inch thickness on a lightly floured surface; cut with a 3-inch round cutter. Place a heaping teaspoon of reserved cherry mixture in center of each cookie; overlap sides, forming a cylinder. Insert a cherry half in each open end. Place 2 inches apart on lightly greased cookie sheets. Repeat procedure with remaining dough. Bake at 400° for 20 to 25 minutes or until lightly browned. Remove from cookie sheets, and cool on wire racks.

Combine sugar, 1 cup water, honey, and lemon juice in a saucepan; bring to a boil. Reduce heat; simmer, uncovered, 15 minutes, stirring occasionally. Cool glaze to room temperature; drizzle over cookies. Let dry completely before serving. Yield: about 2 dozen.

Long abandoned sugar mill at New Smyrna Beach, Florida.

NEW SMYRNA EASTER COOKIES

1 cup butter, softened
½ cup shortening
½ cup vegetable oil
2 cups plus 1 teaspoon sugar,
  divided
½ cup milk
2 eggs
1 teaspoon vanilla extract
6 to 6½ cups all-purpose
  flour, divided
2 tablespoons baking powder
2 egg yolks
¼ cup water
1 cup sesame seeds (optional)

Combine butter, shortening, and oil in a large mixing bowl; beat until well blended. Gradually add 2 cups sugar, beating well. Add milk, 2 eggs, and vanilla; mix well.

Sift together 3 cups flour and baking powder; add to creamed mixture, beating until smooth. Sift remaining flour; gradually stir in enough flour to make a stiff dough.

Roll into 6-inch ropes; shape each rope into a circle, gently pinching ends together to seal. Place on greased cookie sheets.

Combine 2 egg yolks, water, and remaining sugar, beating well. Lightly brush each cookie with egg yolk mixture; sprinkle with sesame seeds, if desired.

Bake at 350° for 15 minutes or until lightly browned. Let cool slightly on cookie sheets; remove to a wire racks to cool completely. Yield: about 9½ dozen.

In 1768, Dr. John Turnbull brought some 1400 indentured colonists, mostly from the Spanish island of Minorca, to a huge tract of land eighty miles south of St. Augustine, Florida. He named the settlement New Smyrna (known as New Smyrna Beach after 1930) in honor of his wife's birthplace. His plan was to grow indigo, but by 1777, incredible hardships had taken such a toll that only a few hundred survivors made it to St. Augustine for refuge. The descendants of those survivors live there today.

HAMANTASCHEN

2¼ cups all-purpose flour
1 cup sugar, divided
1½ teaspoons baking powder
¼ teaspoon salt
⅓ cup shortening
2 eggs, beaten
3 tablespoons honey
1 tablespoon lemon juice
Dried Fruit Filling
1 egg, beaten
1 teaspoon cinnamon

Combine flour, ½ cup sugar, baking powder, and salt in a large mixing bowl; cut in shortening with a pastry blender until mixture resembles coarse meal. Add 2 eggs, honey, and lemon juice; stir well. Divide dough in half. Cover and chill thoroughly.

Roll one half of dough to ⅛-inch thickness on a floured surface, keeping remaining dough chilled until ready to use. Cut with a floured 3-inch round cutter. Place 1 heaping teaspoon of Dried Fruit Filling in center of each circle; fold into a 3-cornered hat shape, pinching edges together to seal. Brush cookies with 1 beaten egg. Combine remaining sugar and cinnamon; sprinkle evenly over cookies.

Place 2 inches apart on greased cookie sheets. Bake at 350° for 15 minutes or until lightly browned. Remove from cookie sheets, and cool completely on wire racks. Yield: about 2½ dozen.

Dried Fruit Filling:

½ cup raisins
½ cup dried apricots
½ cup chopped walnuts
¼ cup honey
1 teaspoon grated lemon rind

Grind together raisins, apricots, and walnuts in a medium mixing bowl. Add honey and lemon rind, stirring well. Yield: about 1 cup.

Hamantaschen (above), baked for Purim, which is celebrated (below) by acting out Esther's triumph over Haman.

ITALIAN CHRISTMAS COOKIES

4½ cups all-purpose flour
2 teaspoons baking powder
1¼ cups shortening
¾ cup sugar
⅓ cup milk
1 teaspoon vanilla extract
3 eggs, well beaten
3 (8-ounce) packages dried figs
Frosting (recipe follows)

Combine flour and baking powder in a large mixing bowl; stir well. Cut in shortening with a pastry blender until mixture resembles coarse meal. Make a well in center of mixture, and set aside.

Combine sugar, milk, and vanilla in a small saucepan. Cook over medium heat, stirring constantly, until sugar dissolves. Remove from heat, and gradually stir in eggs. Pour into reserved flour mixture, stirring just until dry ingredients are moistened.

Knead 3 to 4 times on a lightly floured surface. Roll to ¼-inch thickness; cut into 1½-inch squares. Place a fig in the center of each square; press dough around fig.

Place cookies, seam side down, on greased cookie sheets. Bake at 350° for 12 to 15 minutes. Remove from cookie sheets, and cool completely on wire racks. Spread frosting over tops of cookies. Yield: about 10 dozen.

Frosting:

2 tablespoons butter or margarine, softened
2 cups sifted powdered sugar
2 tablespoons milk
Liquid food coloring

Cream butter in a small mixing bowl; gradually add sugar, beating well. Add milk; beat just until smooth. Tint with food coloring as desired. Yield: frosting for 10 dozen cookies.

Annual Las Posadas *procession, San Antonio's River Walk.*

BIZCOCHOS

2 cups lard, softened
2 cups sugar, divided
2 egg yolks
5 cups all-purpose flour
3 tablespoons ground cinnamon, divided
1 tablespoon anise seeds
1 cup Sauterne or other sweet wine

Cream lard in a large mixing bowl; gradually add 1 cup sugar, beating until light and fluffy. Add egg yolks, one at a time, beating well after each addition.

Combine flour, 1 tablespoon cinnamon, and anise in a medium mixing bowl; stir well. Gradually add to creamed mixture alternately with wine, beginning and ending with flour mixture. Divide dough into fourths. Cover and chill at least 1 hour.

Roll one portion of dough to ½-inch thickness on a lightly floured surface. Cut into assorted shapes, using 2-inch cookie cutters. Place on greased baking sheets. Bake at 350° for 12 minutes or until edges are lightly browned. Cool slightly on cookie sheets.

Combine remaining sugar and cinnamon in a small mixing bowl; dredge warm cookies in mixture. Cool completely on wire racks. Repeat procedure with remaining dough and cinnamon-sugar mixture. Yield: about 6 dozen.

ST. AUGUSTINE
FIESTA BUTTER COOKIES

1 cup butter or margarine,
   softened
1½ cups sifted powdered
   sugar
1 egg
1 teaspoon vanilla extract
½ teaspoon almond extract
2½ cups all-purpose flour
1 teaspoon baking soda
1 teaspoon cream of tartar
Dash of salt
About 1 cup chopped mixed
   candied fruit

Cream butter in a large mixing bowl; gradually add sugar, beating until light and fluffy. Add egg, vanilla, and almond extract; beat until well blended.

Sift together flour, soda, cream of tartar, and salt in a medium mixing bowl; gradually add to creamed mixture, mixing well. Cover and chill 1 hour.

Roll to ¼-inch thickness on a lightly floured surface; cut with a 2-inch round cookie cutter. Sprinkle ½ teaspoon chopped candied fruit over each cookie. Place 2 inches apart on ungreased cookie sheets. Bake at 375° for 8 to 10 minutes. Cool slightly on cookie sheets. Remove from cookie sheets, and cool completely on wire racks. Yield: about 8½ dozen.

When the Minorcans resettled at the edge of St. Augustine, they began to put their indelible stamp on matters cultural and culinary. One custom that did not survive was the Easter Eve serenade when the men would get together and sing under the balconies. The songs were religious, but the choruses were requests for snacks, for which St. Augustine Fiesta Butter Cookies would have been appropriate.

The 1920 reenactment of Ponce de León's 1513 landing at St. Augustine.

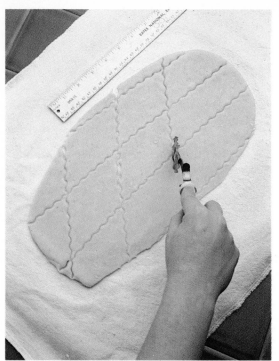

After rolling dough to 1/8-inch thickness, cut into 3- x 2-inch diamonds.

Make a 3/4-inch slit in center of diamonds. Gently pull one corner through as far as possible without tearing.

Fattigmands Bakkelse are the perfect complement to a cup of coffee.

FATTIGMANDS BAKKELSE

¾ cup sugar
2 eggs
8 egg yolks
3 tablespoons brandy
1 cup whipping cream
5 cups all-purpose flour
1 teaspoon ground cardamom
Vegetable oil
Powdered sugar

Combine ¾ cup sugar, eggs, egg yolks, and brandy in a large mixing bowl; beat until thick and lemon colored. Gradually add whipping cream; beat well.

Sift together flour and cardamom in a medium mixing bowl; add to sugar mixture, ½ cup at a time, stirring well after each addition. Cover and refrigerate overnight.

Turn out a small portion of dough onto a lightly floured surface; roll to ⅛-inch thickness. Cut into 3- x 2-inch diamonds; make a ¾-inch lengthwise slit in the center of each, and gently pull one corner through as far as possible without tearing.

Drop 3 to 4 at a time into 4 inches of hot oil (375°). Cook 2 minutes, turning once or until golden brown. Drain on paper towels; sift powdered sugar over tops of cookies. Repeat procedure with remaining dough. Yield: 6 dozen.

HALF-MOONS

1 cup lard
1 cup sugar
2 cups molasses
1 (8-ounce) carton
  commercial sour cream
1½ teaspoons ground
  cinnamon
1½ teaspoons ground allspice
1½ teaspoons ground cloves
1½ teaspoons baking soda
Dash of salt
1 cup chopped pecans
7 cups all-purpose flour

Cream lard in a large mixing bowl; gradually add sugar, beating until light and fluffy. Add molasses, sour cream, spices, soda, and salt; beat well. Stir in pecans. Add flour to form a stiff dough. Divide into 4 equal portions. Cover and chill overnight.

Roll one portion of dough to ¼-inch thickness on a lightly floured surface; keep remaining dough chilled until ready to use. Cut with a half-moon cutter. Place on lightly greased cookie sheets. Bake at 350° for 10 to 12 minutes. Remove from cookie sheets, and cool completely on wire racks. Repeat procedure with remaining dough. Yield: about 15 dozen.

SCANDINAVIAN WREATH COOKIES

¾ cup butter, softened
¾ cup shortening
1 cup plus 2 tablespoons
  sugar, divided
2 eggs
2 teaspoons grated orange
  rind
4 cups all-purpose flour
1 egg white

Cream butter and shortening in a large mixing bowl; gradually add 1 cup sugar, beating until light and fluffy. Add 2 eggs, one at a time, beating well after each addition. Stir in orange rind. Gradually add flour, stirring well after each addition. Chill 1 hour.

Shape into 1-inch balls; roll each ball into a 6-inch rope. Tie each rope into a knot, leaving ½-inch ends. Place 2 inches apart on ungreased cookie sheets; set aside.

Beat egg white (at room temperature) until soft peaks form. Gradually add remaining sugar, 1 tablespoon at a time, beating until stiff peaks form. (Do not underbeat.)

Brush meringue over cookies. Bake at 375° for 8 to 10 minutes. Remove from cookie sheets, and cool on wire racks. Yield: about 8 dozen.

Dancers in Swedish costume, Richmond, Virginia, 1896.

ALSATIAN PLUM COOKIES

¼ cup plus 2 tablespoons shortening
2 cups sugar
3 eggs
1 (8-ounce) package pitted dates
1½ cups chopped pecans
1½ cups raisins
½ teaspoon ground cinnamon
½ teaspoon ground nutmeg
½ teaspoon ground cloves
¼ teaspoon salt
1 teaspoon baking soda
1 tablespoon half-and-half
4 cups all-purpose flour

Cream shortening in a large mixing bowl; gradually add sugar, beating well. Add eggs, one at a time, beating well after each addition.

Grind together dates, pecans, and raisins. Stir fruit mixture, spices, and salt into creamed mixture. Dissolve soda in half-and-half; stir into fruit mixture. Stir in flour to make a stiff dough.

Divide dough into thirds; shape each portion into a roll, 1½ inches in diameter. Wrap rolls in waxed paper, and chill overnight or until firm.

Cut into ¼-inch slices; place 2 inches apart on ungreased cookie sheets. Bake at 350° for 10 to 12 minutes. Remove from cookie sheets, and cool completely on wire racks. Yield: 10 dozen.

ZIMTKRÄNZE

1½ cups butter, softened
1¼ cups sugar, divided
3 eggs, separated
3 to 3½ cups all-purpose flour
1 teaspoon ground cinnamon
1 cup finely chopped pecans

Cream butter in a large mixing bowl; gradually add 1 cup sugar, beating until light and fluffy. Add egg yolks, beating until well blended. Add enough flour to make a stiff dough. Roll to ¼-inch thickness on a floured surface. Cut with a floured 2¾-inch doughnut cutter.

Place 2 inches apart on greased cookie sheets. Brush with lightly beaten egg whites. Combine remaining sugar, cinnamon, and pecans; sprinkle over cookies. Bake at 300° for 15 minutes or until lightly browned. Remove from cookie sheets, and cool on wire racks. Yield: about 5 dozen.

NÜRNBERGER LEBKUCHEN

3 cups honey
2¼ cups firmly packed brown sugar
3 eggs, beaten
1 tablespoon grated lemon rind
3 tablespoons lemon juice
8¼ cups all-purpose flour
1½ teaspoons baking soda
1 tablespoon ground cinnamon
1½ teaspoons ground allspice
1½ teaspoons ground nutmeg
1 teaspoon ground cloves
1 cup diced candied citron
1 cup chopped pecans
Sliced almonds
Glaze (recipe follows)

Bring honey to a boil in a large Dutch oven; remove from heat, and cool slightly. Stir in sugar, beaten eggs, lemon rind, and juice. Combine dry ingredients; gradually add to honey mixture, stirring well. Stir in citron and pecans. Cover mixture and chill overnight.

Shape into 1-inch balls; place 2 inches apart on greased cookie sheets. Dip bottom of a glass in cool water, and gently press balls to ¼-inch thickness. Press an almond slice in center of each cookie. Bake at 400° for 10 minutes. Remove cookie sheets from oven. Brush glaze on cookies, and cool completely on wire racks. Store cookies in airtight containers. Yield: about 14 dozen.

Glaze:

1½ cups sugar
¾ cup water
⅓ cup sifted powdered sugar

Combine 1½ cups sugar and water in a small heavy saucepan; cook over low heat, stirring constantly, until sugar dissolves. Cook over high heat, without stirring, until mixture reaches thread stage (230°). Remove from heat; stir in powdered sugar, mixing well. Place over low heat while cookies are baking to maintain basting consistency. Yield: glaze for 14 dozen cookies.

Buggy ride in German community of Castroville, Texas, c.1900.

Institute of Texan Cultures

Christmas tree hung with intricately decorated cookie

PFEFFERNÜSSE

¾ cup molasses
¾ cup honey
¾ cup shortening
4 cups all-purpose flour
1 teaspoon baking soda
1 teaspoon salt
1 teaspoon ground allspice
1 teaspoon ground mace
½ teaspoon pepper
¼ teaspoon anise seeds,
   crushed
1 egg, beaten
Sifted powdered sugar

Combine molasses and honey in a medium saucepan; cook over low heat until thoroughly heated, stirring frequently. Add shortening; stir until well blended. Remove from heat, and set aside to cool.

Combine flour, soda, salt, allspice, mace, pepper, and anise in a large mixing bowl; stir well. Set aside.

Add egg to cooled molasses mixture, stirring until well blended. Gradually pour into reserved flour mixture, stirring just enough to moisten dry ingredients. Allow dough to rest 15 minutes.

Shape into 1-inch balls, and place 2 inches apart on greased cookie sheets. Bake at 350° for 10 minutes. Remove from cookie sheets, and roll in powdered sugar. Cool on wire racks. Yield: 9½ dozen.

If we consider the good bakeries we've known, chances are they will be German. Wherever Germans settled in the South, bakeries opened and stayed open, some for well over a century so far, like Ehrler's in Louisville. We know where to go for kuchen or a fancy birthday cake. But especially at Christmastime, we know a good German bakery can fill in the gaps in our own baking: Springerles, Zimtsterne, Pfeffernüsse. . . .

German Christmas celebration, Texas, c.1900.

ZIMTSTERNE

3 egg whites
1 cup sugar
2 teaspoons ground
   cinnamon
1 teaspoon grated lemon
   rind
1½ cups unblanched
   ground almonds
2 tablespoons all-purpose
   flour
⅛ teaspoon salt

Beat egg whites (at room temperature) until soft peaks form; gradually add sugar, cinnamon, and lemon rind, beating until stiff peaks form. Remove ½ cup meringue, and set aside. Fold almonds, flour, and salt into remaining meringue.

Roll small amounts of dough at a time to ¼-inch thickness on a heavily floured surface. Cut with a floured star-shaped cutter. Place cookies 2 inches apart on greased cookie sheets. Frost each cookie lightly with reserved meringue. Bake at 300° for 20 to 30 minutes. Remove from cookie sheets, and cool completely on wire racks. Yield: about 3 dozen.

SPRINGERLE

4 eggs
2 cups sugar
1 tablespoon butter,
   softened
2 tablespoons anise seeds,
   crushed
3¾ cups all-purpose flour
½ teaspoon baking powder

Beat eggs in a large mixing bowl until thick and lemon colored; gradually add sugar and butter; continue beating 10 minutes. Stir in anise.

Combine flour and baking powder in a medium mixing bowl; stir well. Add to egg mixture, stirring well.

Roll dough to ⅓-inch thickness on a lightly floured surface. Use a floured cookie mold or springerle rolling pin to imprint dough. Separate cookie squares using a knife. Place 2 inches apart on well-greased cookie sheets. Let stand, uncovered, in a cool, dry place 12 hours or overnight to set design.

Bake at 300° for 12 to 15 minutes. Remove from cookie sheets, and cool on wire racks. Yield: about 4½ dozen.

Springerle dough, springerle rolling pin, and Springerle

SHAPES THAT CELEBRATE

LUCKY LEAVES

½ cup butter or margarine
2 cups firmly packed
  brown sugar
2 eggs, well beaten
1 teaspoon vanilla extract
3 cups all-purpose flour
2 teaspoons baking powder
½ teaspoon salt
½ teaspoon ground nutmeg
¼ teaspoon ground cloves
½ cup cold strong brewed
  coffee
Red hot cinnamon candies
Green maraschino cherries,
  cut into strips

Cream butter in a large mixing bowl; gradually add sugar, beating well. Beat in eggs and vanilla, mixing well.

Sift together flour, baking powder, salt, nutmeg, and cloves 4 times. Stir into creamed mixture alternately with coffee, beginning and ending with flour mixture. Cover and chill overnight.

Divide dough into fourths. Work with one portion of dough at a time, keeping remaining dough chilled until ready to use. Roll to ⅓-inch thickness on a heavily floured surface. Cut with a clover leaf cutter.

Place 1 inch apart on lightly greased cookie sheets. Place 3 cinnamon candies in center of each cookie; place a cherry strip in center as a stem. Bake at 450° for 5 to 7 minutes. Remove from cookie sheets, and cool on wire racks. Repeat procedure with remaining dough. Yield: about 3½ dozen.

A good luck wish on a St. Patrick's Day postcard, 1907.

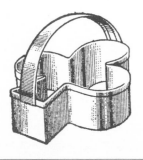

SYMBOL COOKIES

½ cup butter or margarine,
  softened
1 cup sugar
1 egg
2 cups all-purpose flour
2 teaspoons baking powder
½ teaspoon salt
2 tablespoons milk
½ teaspoon vanilla extract

Cream butter in a large mixing bowl; gradually add sugar, beating well. Add egg; beat well.

Combine flour, baking powder, and salt in a medium mixing bowl, mixing well. Add flour mixture, milk, and vanilla to creamed mixture, stirring well. Cover and chill thoroughly.

Roll to ⅛-inch thickness on a floured surface; cut with assorted symbol-shaped cutters. Place on ungreased cookie sheets. Bake at 375° for 6 to 8 minutes. Remove from cookie sheets, and cool on wire racks. Decorate as desired. Yield: about 4½ dozen.

TO-MY-VALENTINE COOKIES

¾ cup butter or margarine,
   softened
¾ cup sugar
1 egg
2 tablespoons milk
1 teaspoon vanilla extract
2½ cups all-purpose flour
1 teaspoon baking powder
½ teaspoon salt
1 cup quick-cooking oats,
   uncooked
Powdered Sugar Frosting

Cream butter in a large mixing bowl; gradually add sugar, beating until light and fluffy. Add egg, milk, and vanilla, and beat well.

Combine flour, baking powder, salt, and oats, stirring well. Add to creamed mixture; stir well. Divide dough in half, and chill thoroughly.

Roll half of dough to ¼-inch thickness on a lightly floured surface; keep remaining dough chilled until ready to use. Cut with a heart-shaped cutter. Place on lightly greased cookie sheets. Bake at 375° for 8 to 10 minutes. Remove from cookie sheets, and cool on wire racks. Repeat procedure with remaining dough. Frost with Powdered Sugar Frosting. Yield: about 3 dozen.

Powdered Sugar Frosting:

2 cup sifted powdered sugar
¼ cup plus 2 tablespoons
   whipping cream
Red food coloring

Combine all ingredients in a small mixing bowl, mixing until smooth. Yield: frosting for 3 dozen cookies.

FRUIT-SHAPED BUTTER COOKIES

1½ cups butter, softened
¾ cup sugar
¼ teaspoon almond extract
3¾ cups all-purpose flour
Liquid Food Coloring

Cream butter in a large mixing bowl; gradually add sugar, beating well. Add almond extract, and beat until well blended. Gradually add flour, stirring well after each addition.

Divide dough into 5 portions, and place each in a small mixing bowl. Tint each portion to desired shade with food coloring. Cover and chill 1 hour.

Mold dough into assorted fruit shapes, using apple stems and whole cloves for blossom ends. Place on ungreased cookie sheets, and bake at 250° for 30 to 35 minutes. Cool slightly on cookie sheets. Carefully remove to wire-meshed racks to cool completely. Yield: about 4 dozen.

Note: These cookies may be used as a garnish for other cookies and cakes.

A heart in bondage on a 1907 St. Valentine's Day card.

Roll dough to ¼-inch thickness. Using a knife, carefully trace the paper pattern onto the cookie dough.

Slowly pipe the fluid white frosting to cover unfrosted area of each cookie. Let the frosting harden.

HOW TO MAKE PATTERN COOKIES

SPOOK COOKIES

1 cup butter or margarine, softened
½ cup sugar
½ cup firmly packed brown sugar
1 egg
3 ounces milk chocolate, melted
1 teaspoon vanilla extract
3¼ cups all-purpose flour
½ teaspoon baking soda
¼ teaspoon salt
Decorator Frosting
Food coloring

Cut several ghost patterns, approximately 4½ inches, from brown paper or parchment. (A round 3½-inch cutter may be used to create desired shapes.)

Cream butter in a large mixing bowl; gradually add sugar, beating until light and fluffy. Add egg, mixing well. Stir in chocolate and vanilla. Combine flour, soda, and salt; add to creamed mixture, stirring well. Chill 1 hour.

Roll to ¼-inch thickness on a lightly floured surface; cut into ghost shapes using the precut paper pattern or a round cutter. Remove paper, and place on greased cookie sheets; bake at 350° for 10 to 12 minutes. Cool slightly on cookie sheets; remove to wire racks to cool completely.

Prepare Decorator Frosting. Tint one-third of frosting to desired color. Pipe frosting around outer edge of each cookie, and form eyes, as desired.

Add water to remaining white frosting to create a more fluid consistency. Pipe to cover unfrosted area of each cookie. Let the frosting harden. Yield: about 2½ dozen.

Decorator Frosting:

½ teaspoon cream of tartar
3 egg whites
1 (16-ounce) package powdered sugar, sifted

Combine cream of tartar and egg whites. Beat at medium speed of an electric mixer until foamy. Gradually add sugar; continue beating 5 to 7 minutes or until stiff peaks form. Yield: frosting for 2½ dozen cookies.

CANDY CANE COOKIES

⅔ cup butter or margarine,
    softened
⅔ cup sugar
1 egg
1 egg yolk
1 teaspoon vanilla extract
2 cups all-purpose flour
½ teaspoon baking soda
¼ teaspoon salt
Red food coloring

Cream butter in a large mixing bowl; gradually add sugar, beating until light and fluffy. Add egg, egg yolk, and vanilla, beating well.

Combine flour, soda, and salt in a small mixing bowl; add to creamed mixture, stirring well. Divide dough in half; tint one half with red food coloring. Wrap each half in waxed paper; chill 2 hours.

Shape into 6- x ¼-inch ropes on a lightly floured surface. Place plain ropes and red ropes together, and twist gently. Place on greased cookie sheets, and shape into candy canes. Bake at 350° for 10 to 12 minutes. Cool slightly on cookie sheets, and remove to wire racks. Repeat procedure with remaining dough. Yield: 3 dozen.

Some home bakers can manage to pull off a Christmas tree completely covered with edible sugarplums. For ideas, just look at the stunning trees used as showpieces on historic home tours; there are always candy canes, for instance. If a whole tree seems too formidable to cover with home-mades, consider an evergreen branch anchored in a bowl of wet sand. Manageable in size, it is easily dressed with just a few dozen Candy Cane Cookies. Children of all ages will behave like birds at a feeder. Have refills standing by!

Cookies emerge from the oven to the utter delight of children . . . then and now.

WHITE CHRISTMAS COOKIES

1½ cups butter, softened
3 cups sifted powdered sugar
4 eggs, well beaten
3 cups all-purpose flour
½ teaspoon salt
1½ teaspoons ground nutmeg
3 tablespoons sherry

Cream butter in a large mixing bowl; gradually add sugar, beating well. Beat in eggs. Sift together flour, salt, and nutmeg three times; gradually add to creamed mixture, stirring well. Stir in sherry. Chill overnight.

Divide dough into fourths. Work with one portion of dough at a time, keeping remaining dough chilled until ready to use.

Roll one portion of dough to ⅛-inch thickness on a lightly floured surface. Cut with assorted shaped cutters; place 1 inch apart on lightly greased cookie sheets. Bake at 350° for 7 minutes. Remove from cookie sheets, and cool on wire racks. Repeat with remaining dough. Yield: about 6½ dozen.

White Christmas Cookies are shown in the cutting stage.

HOLIDAY GINGERBREAD BEARS

1¾ cups sugar
¾ cup honey
¼ cup butter or margarine
1 tablespoon grated lemon rind
⅓ cup lemon juice
6 cups all-purpose flour
¼ cup plus 2 tablespoons baking powder
⅛ teaspoon salt
1½ teaspoons ground ginger
1 teaspoon ground cinnamon
¼ teaspoon ground nutmeg
¼ teaspoon ground cloves
1 egg, well beaten
1 egg yolk, well beaten

Cover 4 cookie sheets with lightly greased waxed paper; set aside.

Combine sugar, honey, and butter in a heavy saucepan. Bring to a boil, stirring constantly until sugar dissolves. Remove from heat; add lemon rind and juice, mixing well. Cool to room temperature.

Combine flour, baking powder, salt, and spices; stir well. Add 2 cups flour mixture, egg, and egg yolk to cooled honey mixture; mix well. Gradually add remaining flour mixture, mixing well. With floured hands, shape dough into a ball, and knead 4 to 5 times on a lightly floured surface.

Divide dough into fourths. Place one fourth on a prepared cookie sheet. Roll to ¼-inch thickness, covering entire cookie sheet. Arrange paper patterns for 1 large, 2 medium, or 6 small gingerbread bears over rolled dough. Cut around patterns with the tip of a knife. Peel away excess dough; combine with remaining dough. Repeat procedure.

Bake at 325° for 20 minutes or until firm and golden brown. Remove from oven; carefully slip a spatula under cookies to loosen. Let cool 1 minute on cookie sheets. Remove to wire racks to cool completely. Yield: 1 dozen large bears, 2 dozen medium bears, or 4 dozen small bears.

A young cook sharing her batch of cookies, c.1902.

ACKNOWLEDGMENTS

Aiken's Row Bourbon Cookies, Brandied Fruit Logs, Butter Crisps, Charleston Vanilla Wafers, Chocolate-Walnut Refrigerator Cookies, Cinnamon Tea Cakes, Crunchy Oatmeal Cookies, Dixie Date Bars, Raspberry Jam Logs, Sea Island Spice Cookies adapted from *Caterin' to Charleston* by Gloria Mann Maynard, Meredith Maynard Chase, and Holly Maynard Jenkins, ©1981. By permission of Merritt Publishing Company, Charleston, South Carolina.

Almond Christmas Cookies, Rolled Sweet Wafers, Christmas Butter Cookies, Coconut Pie Bars, Defense Cookies, Lemon Cookies, Pecan Kiss Cakes adapted from *Charleston Receipts* by The Junior League of Charleston, ©1950. By permission of The Junior League of Charleston, South Carolina.

Almond Icebox Cookies, Applesauce Cookies, Date Pinwheel Cookies, Dutch Butter Cookies, Moravian Tea Cakes, Pecan Crispies, Sour Cream Cookies, Swedish Cookies adapted from *Recipes From Old Virginia*, compiled by The Virginia Federation of Home Demonstration Clubs, ©1958. By permission of The Virginia Extension Homemakers Council, Austinville, Virginia.

Almond Shortbread by Mrs. R.S. Clarke, Glazed Cinnamon Cookies by Mrs. Warren Rendall, Cocoa-Nut Cookies by Mrs. Robert Maurais, Cream Cheese Thumbprint Cookies by Mrs. J.C. Council adapted from *The Gasparilla Cookbook* by The Junior League of Tampa, ©1961. By permission of The Junior League of Tampa, Florida.

Apricot Blondies, Chocolate Caramel Fingers, Christmas Fruit Cookies, Old-Fashioned Sugar 'n Spice Cookies, Sand Dollars, Vanilla Nut Icebox Cookies adapted from *The James K. Polk Cookbook* by The James K. Polk Memorial Auxiliary, ©1978. By permission of The James K. Polk Memorial Auxiliary, Columbia, Tennessee.

Apricot Jewels, Apricot Turnovers, Banana Cake Cookies, Guess-Again Cookies, Gumdrop Cookies, Heavenly Fudge Bars, Orange Slice Bars, Rock Cookies adapted from *Huntsville Heritage Cookbook* by The Grace Club Auxiliary, ©1967. By permission of The Grace Club Auxiliary, Huntsville, Alabama.

Banana Bars, Bird's Nest Cookies, Chewy Blonde Brownies, Cream Cheese Horns, Delta Bars, Double-Dip Nut Fingers, Dream Bars, Hamantaschen, London Bars, Pecan Delights, Toffee Bars adapted from *Keneseth Israel Sisterhood Cookbook* by Keneseth Israel Sisterhood, ©1971. By permission of Keneseth Israel Sisterhood, Louisville, Kentucky.

Bitter Chocolate Cookies, Brazil Nut Macaroons adapted from *Out of Kentucky Kitchens* by Marion Flexner, ©1949. By permission of Franklin Watts, Inc., New York.

Bizcochos adapted from *Seasoned with Sun* by the Junior League of El Paso, Texas, ©1974. By permission of the Junior League of El Paso, Texas.

Breadcrumb Meringue Cookies, Zimtsterne adapted from *Guten Appetit!*, compiled by the Sophienburg Museum, ©1978. By permission of the Sophienburg Museum, New Braunfels, Texas.

Brownies courtesy of Marian Williams, Bartlettsville, Oklahoma.

Buñuelo Rosettes adapted from *Cooking Texas Style* by Candy Wagner and Sandra Marquez, ©1983. By permission of the University of Texas Press, Austin, Texas.

Butter Fingers, Oatmeal-Pecan Lace Cookies, Shortbread adapted from *The Monticello Cookbook* by The University of Virginia Hospital Circle, ©1950. By permission of the Dietz Press, Richmond, Virginia.

Caramel Press Cookies, Chocolate Chip Brownies, Peanut Butter Crunchies adapted from *Welcome Back to Pleasant Hill* by Elizabeth C. Kremer, ©1977. By permission of Shakertown at Pleasant Hill, Harrodsburg, Kentucky.

Cherry Winks, Peanut Blossoms, Starlight Mint Surprise Cookies courtesy of the Pillsbury Company, Minneapolis, Minnesota.

Chocolate Chip Forgotten Cookies, Honey Cookies adapted from *The Bush Family Cookbook*. Courtesy of Mrs. Bob Morris, Dallas, Texas.

Chocolate Rocks, Lucky Leaves, Sour Cream Rocks adapted from *The Treasure Chest of Old Southern Recipes*, published by the millers of LaFrance Flour.

Christmas cards in photograph on page 110 courtesy of Birmingham Museum of Art. Birmingham, Alabama.

Cinnamon Jumbles, Mother Kearney's Sugar-Raisin Cookies adapted from *To Serve with Love* by the Women's Auxiliary of Wheeling Hospital, Wheeling, West Virginia, printed 1975.

Coconut-Orange Squares, Franklin Brownies, Oatmeal-Chocolate Chip Cookies, Old-Fashioned Ginger Snaps adapted from *The Nashville Cookbook* by Nashville Area Home Economics Association, ©1977. By permission of Nashville Area Home Economics Association, Tennessee.

Coconut Vanities adapted from *The Calumet Book of Oven Triumphs!*, 1912.

Crunchy Peanut Bar Cookies, Swedish Rye Cookies adapted from *Swedish Folk Dances Cookbook*, compiled by The Lindsborg Swedish Folk Dancers, Lindsborg, Kansas. Printed in 1979.

Crunchy Skillet Cookies adapted from *Little Rock Cooks* by The Junior League of Little Rock, ©1972. By permission of The Junior League of Little Rock, Inc., Arkansas.

Early American Peanut Cookies adapted from *A Source of Much Pleasure*, edited by Virginia Phillips Holz. By permission of The Mordecai Square Historical Society, Raleigh, North Carolina.

Florentines, Linzer Cookies, New Bern Almond Macaroons, Shortbread Fans, Tryon Palace Ginger Cookies courtesy of Cliff West, New Bern, North Carolina.

Fruitcake Cookies courtesy of Mrs. Bobbie N. Edwards, Grove Hill, Alabama.

German Cream Cheese Brownies adapted from *Revel* by The Junior League of Shreveport, Inc., ©1980. By permission of Books Unlimited, Shreveport, Louisiana.

Gottlieb's Bakery Fruit Bars courtesy of Gottlieb's Bakery, Savannah, Georgia.

Greek Almond Cookies, Greek Holiday Cookies adapted from *Come Cook with Us: A Treasury of Greek Cooking* by The Hellenic Woman's Club, ©1967. By permission of The Hellenic Woman's Club, Norfolk, Virginia.

Half-Moons courtesy of the *Square House Museum Cookbook*. By permission of Carson County Square House Museum, Panhandle, Texas.

Italian Christmas Cookies courtesy of Mrs. Phillip Renda, Trussville, Alabama.

Italian Pillows adapted from *Ozarks Cookery* by Eula Mae Stratton, ©1976. By permission of *The Ozark Mountaineer*, Branson, Missouri.

Juliette Gordon Low Cookies courtesy of Juliette Gordon Low Girl Scout National Center, Savannah, Georgia.

Kentucky Bourbon Cookies adapted from *Famous Kentucky Recipes*, compiled by Cabbage Patch Circle, Louisville, Kentucky.

Kiss Cakes adapted from *Two Hundred Years of Charleston Cooking*, edited by Lettie Gay, ©1976. By permission of the University of South Carolina Press.

Ladyfingers courtesy of *Creative Ideas for Living*, Birmingham, Alabama.

Lemon Squares courtesy of Mrs. Polly Eubanks, Montgomery, Alabama.

Lizzies, Mary Telfair's Derby Cakes, Pumpkin Spice Cookies adapted from *Savannah Sampler Cookbook* by Margaret Wayt DeBolt, ©1978. By permission of The Donning/Company Publishers, Norfolk, Virginia.

Maryland Black Pepper Cookies, Thomas Jefferson's Bachelor Buttons, Waverly Jumbles adapted from *The Presidents' Cookbook* by Poppy Cannon and Patricia Brooks, ©1968. By permission of Funk and Wagnalls.

Mary Randolph's Macaroons adapted from *The Virginia Housewife* by Mrs. Mary Randolph, 1824.

Monticello Macaroons adapted from *Thomas Jefferson's Cookbook*, edited by Marie Kimball, ©1979. By permission of University Press of Virginia, Charlottesville, Virginia.

Mud Hens, Rum Bars, White Christmas Cookies adapted from *The Mississippi Cookbook*, compiled by the Home Economics Division of the Mississippi Cooperative Extension Service. By permission of the University Press of Mississippi, Jackson.

Oma's Sugar Cookies, Springerle, Molasses Cookies courtesy of Peggy Cox, Fredericksburg, Texas.

Original Toll House® Cookies adapted from *Toll House Heritage Cookbook*. Courtesy of Nestlé Company, White Plains, New York.

Passover Macaroons adapted from *Jane Nickerson's Florida Cookbook*, ©1973. By permission of University Presses of Florida, Gainesville.

Peanut Butter Squares adapted from *Fredericksburg Home Kitchen Cookbook*, published by The Fredericksburg Home Kitchen Cookbook Central Committee, 1957. By permission of The Fredericksburg Home Kitchen Cookbook Central Committee, Fredericksburg, Texas.

Raleigh Tavern Oatmeal Cookies courtesy of Raleigh Tavern Bakery, Williamsburg, Virginia.

Rolled Benne Wafers courtesy of Dorothy Barnwell Kerrison, Charleston, South Carolina.

Scandinavian Wreath Cookies adapted from *From Norse Kitchens* courtesy of Our Savior's Lutheran Church Women, Clifton, Texas.

Shaker Vanilla Cookies adapted from *We Make You Kindly Welcome* by Elizabeth C. Kremer, ©1970. By permission of Shakertown at Pleasant Hill, Harrodsburg, Kentucky.

Sheffield Chews courtesy of Mrs. Guy Taliaferro, Sheffield, Alabama.

Stained glass in photograph on page 43 designed by and courtesy of Class Glass, Montgomery, Alabama.

Texas Tea Cakes by Jonelle Thornberry Jordan, Dallas, first appeared in *Cook 'em Horns* by The Ex-Students' Association of the University of Texas, ©1981. By permission of The Ex-Students' Association, Austin.

Walden's Ridge Toll House Sugar Cookies adapted from *Helen Exum's Cookbook*, ©1982. By permission of Helen McDonald Exum, Chattanooga, Tennessee.

Winkler's Ginger Cakes courtesy of Winkler Bakery, Winston-Salem, North Carolina.

 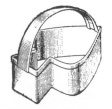 

INDEX

THE Magazine For You if you Share Our Interest in the South.

SOUTHERN LIVING features articles to help make life for you and your family more comfortable, more stimulating, more fun . . .

SOUTHERN LIVING is about your home and how to make a more attractive, more convenient, more comfortable place to live. Each issue brings you dozens of decorating and remodeling ideas you can adapt to your own surroundings.

SOUTHERN LIVING is about gardening and landscaping and how to make the outside of your home just as attractive as the inside. In addition to gardening features, you'll find a monthly garden calendar pinpointing what to plant and when, plus a "Letters to our Garden Editor" section to answer your own particular questions.

SOUTHERN LIVING is about good food and entertaining, with recipes and menu ideas that are sure to delight your family and friends. You'll discover recipes with a Southern accent from some of the South's superlative cooks.

SOUTHERN LIVING is about travel and just plain fun. Every new issue offers an information-packed monthly calendar of special events and happenings throughout the South, plus features on the many fascinating places of interest the South has to offer.

To find out how you can receive SOUTHERN LIVING every month, simply write to: **Southern Living.**
P.O. Box C-119
Birmingham, AL 35283